The Belle & Boo BOOK OF Craft

Illustrations by Mandy Sutcliffe
Photography by Laura Edwards

Quadrille
PUBLISHING

Contents

This is Belle, and this is Boo.
They are always together –
on sunny days,
rainy days,
and dreamy let's-be-lazy days.

Welcome to the enchanted world of Belle and Boo, an idyllic place where the children and animal characters created by illustrator Mandy Sutcliffe live happily together. With this book of 25 projects to make for children, you too can now enter the world of Belle and Boo and bring its unique qualities of warmth, innocence and adventure to your own family life. With a little imagination and the fantastical Pirate Play Tent on pages 116–119 the kitchen table becomes a sea-faring galleon, headquarters for an expedition to search for buried treasure and the Meadow Picnic Blanket on pages 104–107 is a magic carpet that brings a flowery meadow indoors. Belle's Wendy House on pages 42–45 is modelled on her treetop hideout, a dreamy space and the perfect spot to while away lazy hours, drawing and doodling, day dreaming with Boo and other friends. It's something that everyone can share.

As well as her companion and confidant Boo, Belle has many other toy and animal friends. With the instructions on pages 32–37, you can give life to your very own bunny best friend by making a super-huggable Boo soft toy rabbit. Or sew a Pullalong Elephant, an adorable miniature jumbo that your child will never forget, which you can find on pages 88–93. These special toys are sure to become lifelong companions – keepsakes that outlast childhood.

The Patchwork Bedcover on pages 110–113 is another family heirloom. It is a beautiful way to recycle outgrown garments, such as baby's first dress, and other scraps of fabric that have some

special significance or memory attached. Why not involve your little one in the making of this project by getting them to help choose the fabrics and colours, and even counting out the patches.

For those special bake days spent together cooking up tasty treats, make your future chef their very own Little Helper Apron on pages 18–21. Or take a stroll through your local park or woodland to collect some fallen leaves; these can then be identified and used as the leaf templates for the Nature Walk Bunting on pages 24–27. Cutting out simple felt shapes is a good starter project for a young crafter.

You don't have to be an expert stitcher to make all the projects in this book. Some of the ideas involve no more than some cutting and sticking, so even if you have never threaded a needle before you can still make the colourful Hot-Air Balloon Mobile on pages 39–40, the Button Pictures on pages 12–13 and the Kite Rewards Chart on pages 82–83. But for those who are keen to learn new sewing skills, or for anyone who needs a refresher, full instructions are given for the techniques used in the projects on pages 120–123.

The enchanting and inspirational projects in this book will warm your heart and help you to craft a magical world to share with your child, creating something far more valuable than you can ever imagine – a wealth of cherished memories for you to treasure always.

Love, Belle & Boo x

Enchanting
Belle & Boo
PROJECTS

In this section you will find a variety of charming projects to make for your special little one. Inspired by the sweetly nostalgic world of Belle & Boo, the collection of 25 original items includes comforting homewares and stylish accessories, adventurous toys and imaginative play spaces. Create everlasting memories for you and your children with this captivating selection of creative craft projects.

Button Pictures

Sheet of thick card
Sheet of plain pale card
   (to fit the box frame)
Sheet of plain white paper
Sharp pencil
Box frame
Selection of buttons
Glue gun or clear adhesive
Templates: Initials
   (see page 124)

MARKING THE OUTLINE
1 Using the enlarged templates from page 124, trace your chosen initial onto a sheet of thick card. Enlarge the template using a photocopier so that it fits comfortably within the box frame. Cut out the letter carefully from the thick card, position it centrally on the sheet of pale card and lightly draw around the outside edge with a sharp pencil. Repeat with the sheet of white paper.

ARRANGING THE BUTTONS
2 Arrange the buttons within the initial shape on the sheet of white paper. Fill the letter with buttons, grading them from the palest colours at the top, down to the darkest shades at the bottom. Use larger buttons to fill in the bigger, wider spaces and smaller ones for the narrow, more fiddly parts of the letter.

FIXING THE BUTTONS
3 Once you are happy with the placement, transfer the buttons, one at a time, to the corresponding position on the pale card. Fix each with a dab of glue on the back.

4 Once you have filled the initial shape with a single layer of buttons, add depth to the design by adding a second layer.

5 Leave the card lying flat until the glue has dried completely, then place the card and button initial in the box frame.

Pirate Games Beanbag

for a large beanbag
137cm x 110cm furnishing weight
   cotton in 'Pirate Games' print
50cm x 100cm furnishing weight
   plain cotton (for the base and
   the handles)
60cm nylon zip
Cotton jersey beanbag liner
0.5 sq m of polystyrene beads

for a small beanbag
137cm x 60cm furnishing weight
   cotton in 'Classic Belle & Boo'
   print
30cm x 100cm furnishing weight
   plain cotton (for the base and
   the handles)
40cm nylon zip
Cotton jersey beanbag liner
0.25 sq m of polystyrene beads

Dressmaker's squared paper
Matching sewing thread
Basic sewing kit

CUTTING OUT
FOR A LARGE BEANBAG
from 'Pirate Games' cotton
   One 62cm diameter circle
   (for the top)
   Two 98cm x 40cm rectangles
   (for the sides)

from plain cotton
   Two 62cm diameter half circles
   (for the base)
   Four 30cm x 8cm curved handles

FOR A SMALL BEANBAG
from 'Classic Belle & Boo' cotton
   One 40cm diameter circle
   (for the top)
   Two 60cm x 25cm rectangles
   (for the sides)

from plain cotton
   Two 40cm diameter half circles
   (for the base)
   Four 22cm x 6cm curved handles

SAFETY FIRST *Use polystyrene beads
with a flame retardant additive, that
meet current industry standards.*

TIPS *Soft leather makes a luxurious
alternative for the handles. If you
can't find the right length zip, buy
a longer one and trim it to size.*

MAKING THE PATTERN
Follow the same steps for both beanbag
sizes. Draw the circle and rectangle
pattern pieces onto dressmaker's squared
paper, using a pair of compasses to trace
the circle. Once you've cut out the top
circle, fold the pattern piece in half and
mark a line 15mm from the crease. Use
this to cut the two base half circles, cutting
a straight edge along the marked line.

ASSEMBLING THE BASE
1 Turn back and press a 2cm hem along
the straight edges of both base half circles.
Open the zip and tack the zip tapes to
the backs of the hems, making sure the
two halves form a circle. Using a zip foot,
stitch along each straight edge, 3mm from
the folds. Stitch across both ends of the
zip to keep the sides together. If necessary,
trim any excess from the zip.

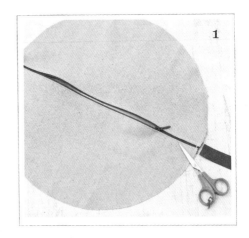

MAKING THE HANDLES

2 With wrong sides facing, pin two handles together. Leaving a 5cm gap along one straight side, stitch around the outside, 1cm from the edge. Apart from by the gap, trim the seam back to 4mm. Turn back and press the trimmed seam so it is in line with the stitches.

3 Turn the handle right side out and ease out the seams. Tack the two sides of the opening together to close. Top stitch around the handle, 4mm from the edge. Make both handles in the same way.

PREPARING THE SIDES

4 With right sides facing, pin the two rectangles together along both short sides. Stitch together with a 1.5cm seam, then press the seam open. Turn right side out.

5 Pin the ends of one handle either side of one of the side seams. The top curve of the handle should be in line with the top raw edge of the side. Sew down around the bottom 3cm on each curved end, stitching a cross to reinforce them.

PUTTING IT ALL TOGETHER

6 With the wrong side out, fold the sides in half so that the seams are outermost. Fold the sides in half a further three times to make eight equal divisions. Mark each end of the folds with a pin around the top and bottom edges.

7 Fold the top and base circles in half four times and mark the fold ends with pins. With right sides facing, match the left and right edges of the top circle to the top of the seams on the sides. Pin around the rest of the circle, matching the marker pins.

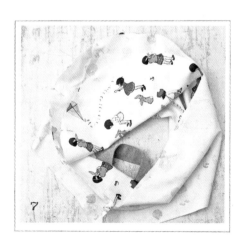

8 Make a round of 1cm deep snips, spaced 2cm apart, into the top edge of the sides so the fabric will stretch around the circumference of the top. Tack together.

9 Open the zip and attach the base circle to the sides in the same way as the top. Stitch around the top and bottom edges with a 1.5cm seam. Turn right side out and press lightly. Fill the beanbag liner with polystyrene beads, push into the cover and then do up the zip.

Little Helper Apron

45cm x 50cm cream linen
30cm x 20cm cotton poplin
   in 'Classic Belle & Boo'
   print (select an area with an
   interesting image for the pocket)
Air-erasable fabric pen
Large embroidery hoop
Stranded cotton embroidery
   thread in warm brown,
   mid-brown and steel blue
3m of 2cm-wide bias binding
Dressmaker's squared paper
Matching sewing thread
Basic sewing kit
Template: Utensils (see page 125)

CUTTING OUT
FOR THE APRON

Enlarge the apron pattern by 435% to its full size on some dressmaker's squared paper. You may have to photocopy once by 400% and then again by 135%. Fold the cream linen in half and pin the pattern piece along the fold as indicated. Cut out.

FOR THE POCKET

Cut a 20cm x 14cm pocket from the cotton poplin, selecting an area with an interesting part of the printed design or favourite motif.

EMBROIDERING THE UTENSILS

1 Trace or photocopy the utensil template and using an air-erasable fabric pen, transfer the template onto the apron. Position the utensil template in the centre of the apron front, making sure that there is enough room for the pocket. Place inside an embroidery hoop, pulling the fabric taut. Using three strands of embroidery thread, back stitch over the outlines, working the spoon in warm brown, the fish slice and sauce spoon in mid-brown and the whisk in steel blue.

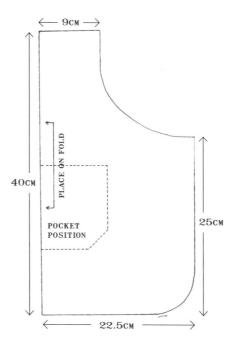

← 9CM →

PLACE ON FOLD

40CM

25CM

POCKET
POSITION

← 22.5CM →

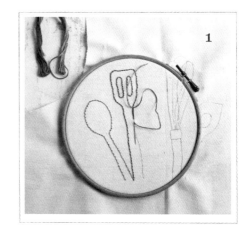

PREPARING THE POCKET

2 Press a 1cm turning along both sides and the bottom edge of the pocket fabric. Fold back both of the bottom corners, to hide the pointed corners and create a diagonal edge.

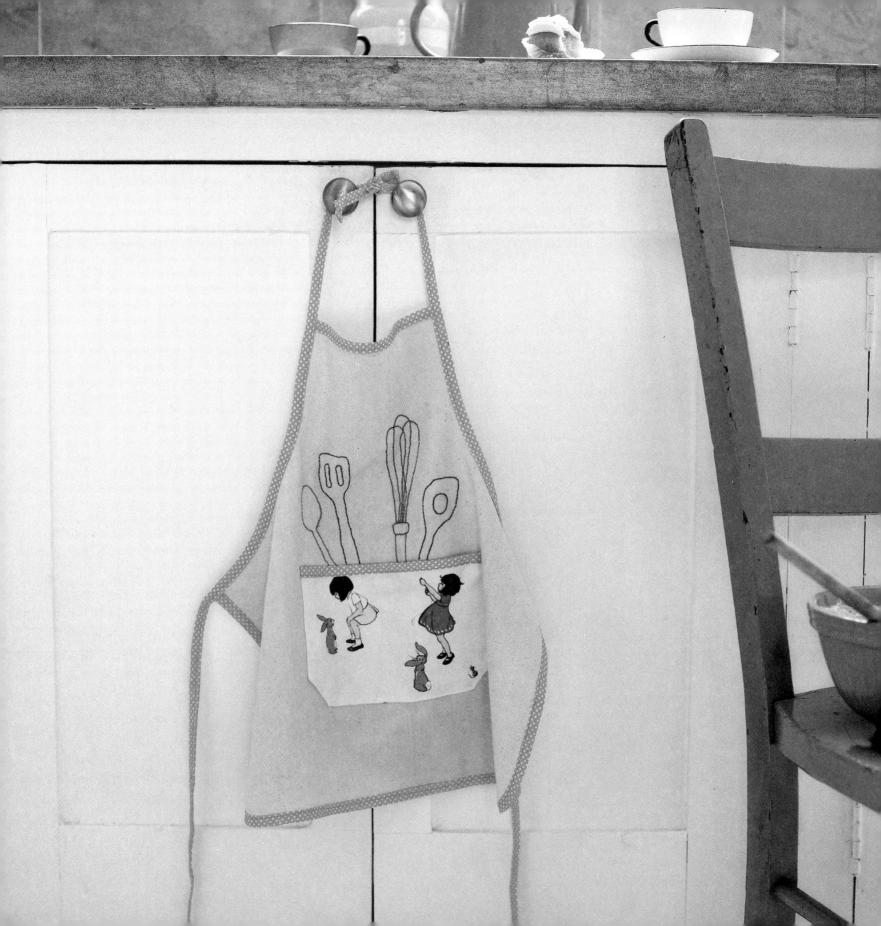

3 Cut a 20cm length of bias binding. Fold it in half lengthways and slot over the top edge of the pocket, so that there is an extra 1cm at each end. Tack in place, then stitch 3mm from the inside edge in a matching thread. Fold back the excess binding at the ends and hand stitch to the wrong side of the pocket.

SEWING ON THE POCKET

4 Using the placement guide, pin the pocket to the apron front so that it hides the bottom of the utensils. Tack in place. Sew from the top of one side to the other, about 5mm in from the edge, either by hand or by machine. Leave the top open.

BINDING THE APRON

5 Bind the edge at the neck of the apron in the same way as the pocket (see step 3). Trim any excess away from the ends so that it is flush with the sides.

6 Starting at the top right corner of the short straight side, tack the bias binding around the short sides and the bottom edge of the apron. When you reach the bottom corners, gently stretch the outside fold of the binding so that it fits comfortably around the curves. Stitch in place by hand or machine. Trim the ends.

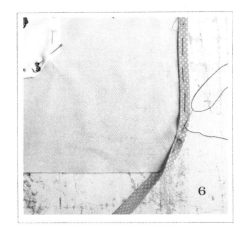

7 Cut the remaining length of binding in half. Leave a 35cm length free and, starting at the bottom edge, pin one of the pieces of binding around one of the armhole curves up to the neck edge. You will need to ease the inside edges of the binding so that it fits inside the curve. You should be left with a length of binding at the neck edge to create a neck tie. Repeat with the second length of binding on the other side.

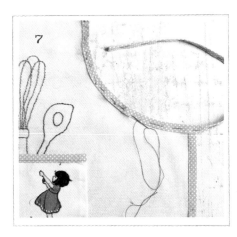

8 Turn and press under 1cm of the ends of the loose binding ties. Press the loose ties in half lengthways and tack in place along the whole length. Machine or hand stitch down using matching thread.

9 Knot the four ends of the binding. Tie the top two ends together to make an adjustable neck loop.

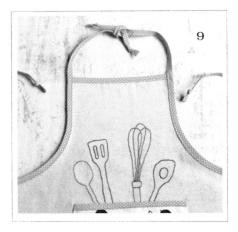

Nature Walk Bunting

Scraps of cotton fabric in a
selection of different colours
and prints
Craft felt in several different
shades of green
Fusible bonding web
Felted wool (see Boo soft toy
on page 32 for instructions
on how to felt wool) in light
and dark brown
Matching sewing thread
Coloured string or yarn
Safety standard toy stuffing
Length of bias binding,
12mm wide
Basic sewing kit
Templates: Pennants, leaves
and acorns (see page 126)

*To make the leaves you can either use
the templates on page 126 or take
your little one on a stroll through
the local park to collect a variety
of fallen leaves. While they are still
fresh, flatten with a heavy book and
then photocopy or trace around the
outline to create your own templates.*

STITCHING A PENNANT

1 Using the template from page 126, cut
two pennants from one of the scraps of
cotton fabric, line up and pin together
with right sides facing.

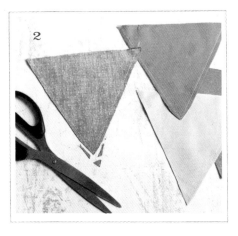

2 Machine stitch along the two longer
edges of the triangle, leaving a 6mm seam
allowance. Clip a small triangle off of the
three triangle points, about 2mm from the
stitch line. This will give the pennant a
neat point when turned right side out.

3 Turn the pennant right sides out.
Ease out the tip using a blunt pencil
and press the seams lightly. Trim off
any pieces of the fabric that protrude
above the open top edge.

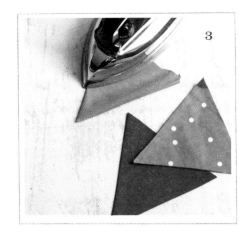

Making an oak leaf

3 Photocopy or trace the large oak leaf template on page 126 or use your own leaves collected on a nature walk. Cut out around the outside edge and use the template to cut out around the large leaf from the green felt.

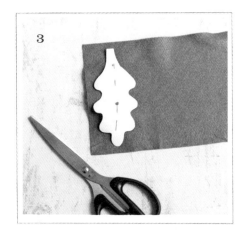

4 Trace the inner outline of the leaf onto the paper side of the bonding web and roughly cut out. Following the manufacturer's instructions, press the adhesive side onto a contrasting green felt using a warm, dry iron. Cut out around the pencil line.

5 Peel the backing paper off the inner leaf. Turn over the main leaf so that the right side is facing upwards and position the inner leaf on top. Press in place with a warm, dry iron and using a pressing cloth.

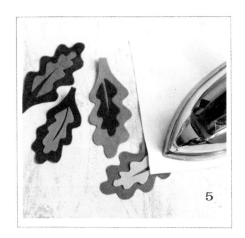

Sewing an acorn

6 Using the three templates on page 126, cut out an 'acorn core' and an 'acorn cover' from light brown felted wool and a 'cup' from dark brown felted wool.

7 Roll up the acorn core along the length of the fabric and, using matching thread, sew down the short edge to keep it tightly rolled. Sew a line of running stitches all the way around the edge of the acorn cover and slightly pull the thread to draw up the sides.

8 Slip the cover over the core and pull the thread until tight. Tie off the thread and make a few stab stitches through the acorn to keep the cover taut.

9 Cut a 10cm loop of string. Fold it in half and make a double knot about 2cm from the fold. Make a small hole in the centre of the acorn cup and feed the loop through it. Secure the loop with a few stitches on the inside.

10 Gather up the acorn cup as for the cover in step 7. Add a small amount of toy stuffing to fill out the base and fit it over the bottom of the acorn, hiding the cover stitching. Sew firmly in place around the gathered edge.

11 Cut a tiny 6mm x 12mm rectangle from the dark brown felted wool, fold it in half and sew it to the top of the acorn.

ASSEMBLING THE BUNTING
For every metre of bunting, you will need 6 pennants, 15 leaves and 5 acorns.

12 Place the first pennant over the wrong side of the bias binding, 10cm in from the end. Line up the top edge of the pennant with the centre line of the binding. Pin in place, then fold over the binding to enclose the raw edge of the pennant and tack in place through all the layers.

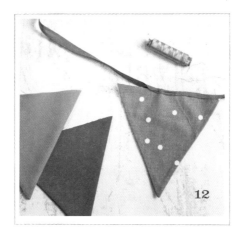

13 Sew two or three leaves in different colour combinations onto the binding, then add another pennant. Continue to within 10cm of the other end, alternating the leaves and the pennants.

14 Using matching thread, sew along the folded edge of the binding either by hand or machine. Add the acorns at random intervals between the leaves, securing them in place with a few stitches.

Playtime Headdress

60cm x 4cm strip of corrugated
   cardboard (the corrugations
   should run widthways)
Clear adhesive
30cm x 10cm green craft felt
Pencil and ruler
Fusible bonding web
15cm x 10cm red craft felt
Pinking shears
60cm length of light yellow
   ric rac
7 buttons, 12mm in diameter
Contrasting sewing thread
10 long feathers
Double-sided tape
Basic sewing kit

CUTTING OUT
from green felt
Two 30cm x 4cm strips

COVERING THE HEADBAND
1 Coat one side of the cardboard strip with a thin layer of adhesive. Fix on the two green felt strips so that they meet in the middle and entirely cover the card. Leave until completely dry.

DRAWING UP THE TRIANGLES
2 Draw a line of seven 3cm x 6cm triangles onto the paper side of the bonding web. Following the manufacturer's instructions, attach the bonding web to the red felt using a pressing cloth to protect the fabric. Cut along the pencil lines with pinking shears.

BONDING THE TRIANGLES

3 Peel the backing paper from the triangles. Place the first triangle, with the point facing downwards and the straight side aligned with the edge of the headband, over the join of the two green pieces of felt. Using a pressing cloth, press it in place with a hot iron. Add three more triangles to each side, alternating the direction of the point of the triangle. Leave a 3cm gap between each.

ADDING THE RIC RAC

4 Starting at the left edge of the headband, run a line of glue between the triangles. Leave until it is almost dry, then stick on the ric rac. Fold the ric rac at a right angle at the outside edge of each zigzag. Stick the loose ends down on the wrong side of the headband.

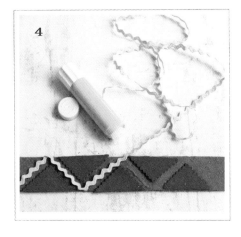

SEWING ON THE BUTTONS

5 Sew a button over the ric rac folds, hiding the bend. Using a contrasting colour, sew through the cardboard.

FIXING THE FEATHERS

6 Starting in the middle of the cardboard, push the feathers into the corrugations of the cardboard, spacing them 2cm apart.

7 Adjust the headdress to fit and secure the ends together with double-sided tape or glue.

Boo

50cm x 50cm fawn felted wool
15cm x 25cm cream felted wool
10cm x 15cm pink felted wool
  or craft felt
5cm x 5cm white fake fur
2 black safety toy eyes,
  1cm in diameter
2 pipe cleaners, 20cm long
Matching sewing thread
Dark brown stranded cotton
  embroidery thread
Black buttonhole thread or fine
  black cotton yarn
Safety standard toy stuffing
4 plastic toy joints,
  2cm in diameter
Small tapestry needle
Basic sewing kit
Templates: Boo (see pages
  127–129)

Boo is made from a recycled, 100% wool jumper. Launder the old knitwear on your hottest washing cycle to shrink them down to a dense felted fabric that will not fray.

CUTTING OUT

Photocopy the templates on pages 127–129 to make your paper patterns.

from fawn felted wool
  2 side heads, 1 reversed
  1 head gusset
  2 ears, 1 reversed
  2 bodies, 1 reversed
  4 arms, 2 reversed
  4 legs, 2 reversed
  2 soles

from cream felted wool
  2 side snouts, 1 reversed
  1 top snout
  2 eyes, 1 reversed
  1 underbelly

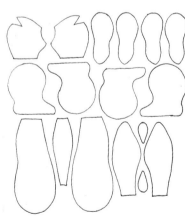

CUTTING GUIDE

from pink felted wool
  2 inner ears, 1 reversed
  1 nose

from white fake fur
  1 tail

Mark and then pierce the positions for the two safety eyes on the two side heads and the eyes, along with the positions for the four washers on both bodies, on two of the arms and two of the legs.

MAKING BOO'S HEAD

1 Line up and stitch the two side snouts to the side head pieces by hand, using small oversew stitches. Push the stems of the safety eyes through the pierced holes in the cream eyes, then through the head. Secure the washers following the manufacturer's instructions and stitch around the cream eyes. Sew the top snout to the tip of the head gusset.

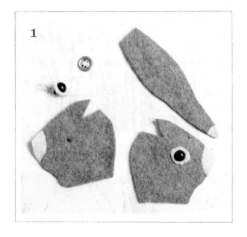

2 Turn back 1cm at the end of each pipe cleaner, then fold them both in half so that they are 9cm in length. Bind the ends with thread to hold in place and conceal any sharp wires. Place one pipe cleaner centrally along the left ear, then pin the left inner ear on top. Stitch around the edge of the inner ear to hold the two together. Repeat with the right ear.

3 Fold the left ear in half widthways, enclosing the pink inner ear. Pinch together the bottom straight edge, overstitching to secure. With the plain, folded side facing outwards, pin the base of the ear to the left side head, aligning so that it points downwards and lies along the lower edge of the dart. Oversew, then fold the top edge of the other dart over to enclose the stitching of the ear. Sew securely through all four layers. Add the right ear to the right side of the head in the exact same way.

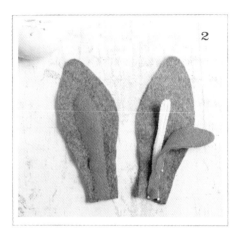

4 Join the two side heads by sewing one to each side of the head gusset, lining up the snout of the head gusset with the side snouts and stitching from the back of the neck to the nose. Sew the inside edges of the ears to the top of the head in line with the gusset seam, this will ensure that they stand upright.

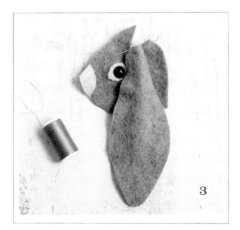

EMBROIDERING BOO'S FEATURES

5 Sew the nose in place, following the guidelines on the pattern on page 128. Using all six strands of the brown embroidery thread, outline the bottom edge of the nose with two straight stitches, then embroider a straight line down from the middle point and embroider two curved lines from this point for the mouth. Add a smattering of French knots on each side of the snout. Define the eyes with two small straight stitches at the outer corners. The whiskers are made from strands of black buttonhole thread securely stitched into the snout. Fill the head firmly with the safety toy stuffing.

ATTACHING BOO'S LEGS

6 Sew a sole to the base of one pierced leg piece, matching points A and B as according to the pattern on page 129. Pin and stitch on a second non-pierced leg piece, leaving the space between C and D open. Stuff the foot and lower leg.

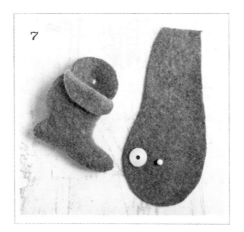

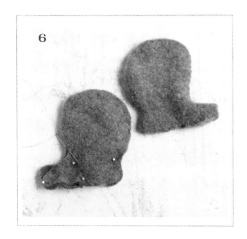

7 Push the pointed end of a toy joint through the hole of the leg, then through the corresponding hole in the lower end of a body piece, ensuring that the leg points forward. Fix on the washer following the manufacturer's instructions. Sew up half of the gap at the top of the leg, filling the remaining space with safety toy stuffing, then close up the gap. Attach the other leg to the second body piece in the same way.

ADDING BOO'S ARMS

8 Sew together one pierced arm piece with one non-pierced arm piece, between points A and B as marked on page 129. Stuff the lower part of the arm with toy stuffing. Push the pointed end of a toy joint through the hole, then through the corresponding hole in the upper end of a body piece, ensuring that the arm points forward. Add the washer following the manufacturer's instructions and finish off as for the leg. Attach the other arm to the second upper body piece in the same way.

SEWING BOO TOGETHER

9 Pin the underbelly to the front edge of one body piece, from point A down to B as marked on pages 127–128. Stitch along this seam, then add the other body piece in the same way. Join the back seam from point B back up to the middle of the back of the neck. Fill firmly with toy stuffing.

10 Centrally line the head up over the neck opening and pin onto the body. Sew the head securely in place. To make sure it holds in place, start and finish the seam securely, use mattress or overstitch and draw up tightly. If you like, work two rounds of stitches for added security.

ADDING THE FINISHING TOUCHES

11 Sew a line of small running stitches around the outside edge of the circle of white fur. Gently gather it up and fill with a small amount of safety toy stuffing to make the tail. Finish off the thread securely and sew the tail in place.

12 Using all six strands of dark brown embroidery thread, work three straight stitches at the end of the arms and legs to indicate Boo's claws.

Hot-Air Balloon Mobile

25cm diameter wooden
  embroidery hoop
  (inner ring only)
Six 50cm lengths of invisible
  thread or fishing line
A4 sheets of heavyweight
  (240gsm) coloured paper in
  a selection of colours
Scissors or craft knife
Glue stick or double-sided tape
Templates: Hot-air balloon, cloud
  and birds (see page 130)

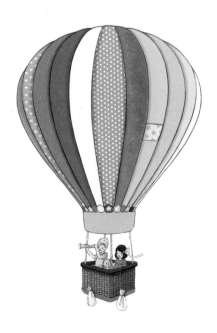

1 Using the template on page 130, trace and cut out the balloon shapes from your coloured paper. You will need to cut 10–12 identical shapes for each balloon. Fold each shape in half lengthways.

2 Using the templates, trace and cut out the clouds from white paper and the birds from blue. For these flat objects, cut two identical shapes for the front and back. To assemble, place some thread between two matching shapes and glue together.

3 To assemble the three-dimensional hot-air balloons: join two matching shapes together by sticking the right half of one to the left half of another. Make sure the edges are lined up. Continue to join the shapes, then – before fixing the final pair of shapes – insert a length of thread for hanging and stick to hold in place.

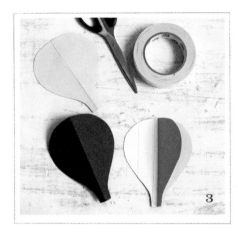

4 Cut a thin strip of coloured paper. Wrap and fix around the base of the completed balloon to help it keep its shape.

5 Glue the two- and three-dimensional objects to the lengths of thread, leaving 25cm of the thread clear at the end.

6 When all your objects have been stuck to your lengths of thread, tie the top ends around your embroidery hoop and secure with a double knot. Make sure that the items are evenly spaced and balanced around the hoop to ensure that it will hang correctly.

7 Use thread or ribbon to hang your mobile from the ceiling.

Belle's Wendy House

140cm x 140cm white cotton
136cm x 3.5m red cotton
80cm x 40cm black cotton
60cm x 40cm purple spot print cotton
60cm x 80cm lilac cotton
80cm x 50cm yellow cotton
30cm x 10cm light green cotton
60cm x 30cm mid-green cotton
30cm x 35cm pale yellow cotton
Assortment of pink, purple and red cotton scraps, totalling 1m x 1m square
3.5m x 3.5m fusible bonding web
40cm length of 2cm-wide webbing
Four 2cm D-rings
Matching sewing thread
Basic sewing kit
Templates: Roof tiles, window box, foliage, flowers and leaves (see page 131)

Hang Belle's Wendy House over a length of washing line in the garden to create the perfect play tent.

CUTTING OUT

from white cotton
Two 135cm x 68cm rectangles (for the roof)

from red cotton
Two 136cm x 150cm rectangles (for the house front and back)
One 35cm x 8cm strip (for the door window)
One 30cm x 8cm strip (for the door window)
Two 35cm x 10cm strips (for the sides of the door window)
One 43cm x 10cm strip (for the top of the door)
One 45cm x 35cm rectangle (for the lower door)

from black cotton
Two 35cm x 35cm squares (for the windows)
One 30cm x 35cm rectangle (for the door window)

from purple spot print cotton
Four 15cm x 35cm rectangles (for the window curtains)

from yellow cotton
Eight 35cm x 8cm strips (for the frame bars)
Two 50cm x 25cm strips (for the window lintel)
Two 75cm x 10cm strips (for the door frame)
One 55cm x 25cm rectangle (for the door lintel)

from pale yellow cotton
Two 15cm x 35cm strips (for the door curtains)

PLACEMENT GUIDE

ASSEMBLING THE ROOF

1 Make a double 2cm hem along the bottom edge of both white roof pieces. Press under and then unfold a 2cm double turning at each short side edge.

2 Trace 64 tiles and 16 lower half tiles onto bonding web. Following the manufacturer's instructions, cut out roughly, press onto the pink, purple and red tile fabrics, then cut out neatly. Cut 4 tiles and 1 lower half tile in half vertically.

3 Make both sides of the roof in the same way, varying the colours in each row. Starting 1cm from the innermost fold on the left side and 3cm from the bottom edge, press down a left half tile. Finish the row with 7 whole tiles and a right half tile.

4 Neaten the lower edges of the tiles with a line of red zigzag stitch. Now add another row of tiles, this time use eight whole tiles to cover the gaps left by the tiles below, overlapping the edges. Again zigzag around the bottom edge. Repeat for another two rows and then finish with a row of lower half tiles along the top edge.

5 Fold over the side hems to conceal the raw edges of the tiles. Pin down and stitch 3mm from the inner fold.

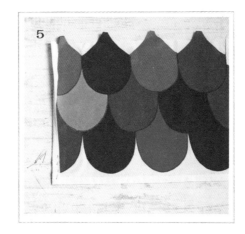

6 Pin the two sides of the roof together along the top edge of half tiles, with right sides facing. Stitch a 2cm seam allowance (see page 122) and press the seam open.

MAKING THE WINDOW

7 Hem one long edge of each curtain and press in 3 pleats. Tack the raw edges to the sides of the window and sew the hems in place. Press a 2cm turning under both long edges of two frame bars. Stitch one down the window centre and add the other widthways to make a cross.

8 Press two frame bar strips in half lengthways. Line up and pin down the raw edges of the bars with the raw edges of the sides of the window and sew in place with a 1cm seam. Press the bars out.

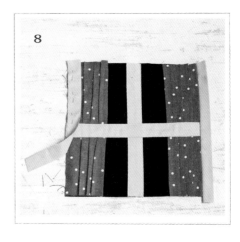

ADDING THE WINDOW LINTEL

9 Press under a 1.5cm turning at each short edge of the window lintel, then fold it in half lengthways and press.

10 Trace six size '3' leaves and two size '3' flowers onto bonding web. Press the leaves onto light green fabric and the flowers onto pink. Trim around the outlines and remove the paper backing.

With the folded edge of the lintel at the top and right side up, press three leaves to the right side of each corner of the lintel (see the placement guide on page 42) and zigzag over the edges with green thread. Iron the flowers over the top and edge with pink thread.

11 With right sides facing, line up and pin the lintel to the top of the window and stitch in place with a 1.5cm seam. Open out and press the lintel upwards so that it sits above the window.

Sewing the window box
12 Using the template on page 131, draw the outline of the window box foliage onto mid-green cotton. Trace and cut out eleven size '1' flowers and nine assorted leaves onto bonding web. Press the flowers onto the roof tile offcuts and the leaves onto light green cotton. Peel off the backing papers, arrange them within the outline and press in place. Zigzag around all the edges in matching thread.

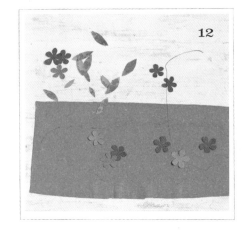

13 Iron a sheet of bonding web to the back of the mid-green cotton and cut out around the outline. Cut the window box from lilac cotton and press a 6mm turning along the sides and the bottom edge. Following the placement guide on page 42, pin the window to the front of one red house piece. Now pin the window box and the foliage in place.

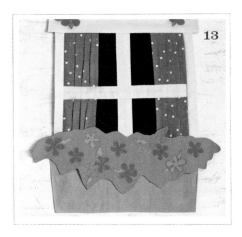

14 Make a second window and pin to the centre of the back of the house.

Making the door
15 Make up the door window as before (see step 7), using pale yellow curtains and red frame bars. Hem one long edge of each curtain and press in three pleats. Tack the raw edges to the sides of the window and sew the hems in place. Press a 2cm turning under both long edges of two frame bars. Stitch one down the window centre and add the other widthways to make a cross.

16 With right sides facing, pin and stitch the top red door strip to the top edge of the window with a 1cm seam allowance. Fold the door strip back and press. Again with right sides facing, pin and stitch the bottom red door piece to the bottom edge of the window using a 1cm seam allowance. Fold back and press flat.

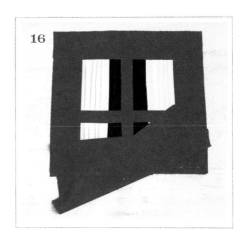

ADDING THE DOOR LINTEL

18 Press under 1cm at each side of the door lintel, then fold in half lengthways and press. Draw on the stem outlines following the placement on page 42. Using the templates on page 131, trace two size '1' flowers, two '2's and one '3', plus four size '1' leaves, eleven '2's and four '3's onto bonding web. Press the leaves onto light green fabric and the flowers onto tile offcuts. Peel off the backing, arrange on the lintel and press. Zigzag around all the edges in matching thread.

17 Press two yellow door frame strips in half lengthways. Line up the raw edges with the raw edges of the sides of the door and pin down. Sew in place with a 1cm seam. Open out and press the frames flat.

19 With right sides facing, line up and pin the lintel to the top of the door and stitch in place with a 1.5cm seam. Open out and press the lintel so that it sits above the door. Pin the door next to the window, so that the lintels are in line with each other. When you are happy with the placement, sew down the door, the front window and window box and the back window using large straight stitches. Press the window box foliage in place and edge using a green zigzag stitch.

20 Press over and stitch a 3cm double hem along the bottom edge of the house, so that it covers the raw edge of the door. Do the same at both side edges.

MAKING UP

21 With wrong sides facing, sew the front and back houses together along the top edge with a 2cm seam. Press the seam open and lay on a flat surface. Position the roof, right side up, on top of the join so that there is an equal overlap at each edge and the two middle seams are aligned. Tack, then stitch along the seam line.

ADDING THE ANCHOR LOOPS

22 Cut the webbing into four 10cm lengths. Thread each one through a D-ring. Slip the ends of the webbing into an opening at the bottom of the side hems. Pin in place and stitch through all the layers to secure.

Pompom Beret

YOU WILL NEED

4ply wool or wool-blend yarn,
   such as Debbie Bliss
   Baby Cashmerino
MC   1 x 50g ball in teal
CC   1 x 50g ball in ecru
A set of five 2.75mm and
   3.25mm double pointed
   knitting needles
Tapestry needle
Cardboard
Scissors

SIZE
To fit age   2–4   4–6   6–8 years

TENSION
32 stitches and 32 rows to 10cm square
over stocking stitch on 3.25mm needles.

ABBREVIATIONS
MC   main colour
CC   contrast colour
k   knit
p   purl
inc   increase by working into front and
       back of the same stitch
dec   decrease by working two stitches
       together at the same time
sts   stitches

MAKING THE BERET
Using 2.75mm double pointed needles and
CC yarn, cast on 104 (112: 118) sts.
Arrange the stitches evenly over four
needles and with the fifth needle join the
stitches in a round, making sure they are
not twisted, and continue as follows:
Round 1: * K1, p1; repeat from * to end
of round.
Change to MC yarn and work Round 1
a further 3 times.
Inc round: * K2, work inc into next 5 sts;
repeat from * to last 6 (0: 6) sts, work inc
into next 6 (0: 6) sts. *180 (192: 204) sts.*
Change to a set of five 3.25mm needles.
Knit 27 (28: 29) rounds.
1st dec round: * K4, k2tog; repeat from *
to end of round. *150 (160: 170) sts.*
Knit 13 rounds.
2nd dec round: * K4, k3tog, k3; repeat
from * to end of round. *120 (128: 136) sts.*
3rd dec round: * K3, k3tog, k2; repeat
from * to end of round. *90 (96: 102) sts.*
4th dec round: * K2, k3tog, k1; repeat
from * to end of round. *60 (64: 68) sts.*
5th dec round: * K1, k3tog; repeat from *
to end of round. *30 (32: 34) sts.*
6th dec round: * K2tog; repeat from * to
end of round. *15 (16: 17) sts.*
Break off the yarn leaving a long end.
Thread the yarn end through the
remaining 15 (16: 17) stitches.
Draw the yarn up to gather the stitches
tightly and secure the end of the yarn to
the reverse side of the hat.

MAKING THE POMPOM

1 Cut two identical circles of card that are slightly smaller than the pompom you need. Cut matching holes in the centre of each circle and then hold them together.

2 Thread a tapestry needle with CC yarn and wind it continually through the centre and over outer edges of the card circles until the centre hole is completely closed.

3 Insert the tips of a pair of scissors between the outer edges of the two card circles and cut between and around them.

4 To secure the pompom, tie a length of yarn tightly between the two card circles, then carefully remove the cardboard.

5 To neaten, trim any loose ends. Secure to the crown of the beret with a length of yarn fixed to the reverse of the hat.

Snowflake Mittens

4ply wool or wool blend yarn,
   such as Debbie Bliss
   Baby Cashmerino
MC   1 x 50g ball in teal
CC   1 x 50g ball in ecru
A set of five 2.75mm and
   3.25mm double pointed
   knitting needles
Stitch holder
Tapestry needle
Cardboard
Scissors

SIZE

To fit age	2–3	4–5	6–7 years
Width	6.5cm	7cm	7.5cm
Length	14cm	14cm	14cm

TENSION

32 stitches and 32 rows to 10cm square
over stocking stitch on 3.25mm needles

ABBREVIATIONS

MC   main colour
CC   contrast colour
k   knit
p   purl
inc   increase
dec   decrease
PM   place marker
SM   slip marker
M1L   make one – left slant: with
lefthand needle, lift the strand running
between the needles from front to back,
then knit the lifted loop through the back
M1R   make one – right slant: with
lefthand needle, lift the strand running
between the needles from back to front,
then knit the lifted loop through the front

MAKING THE MITTENS

Using 2.75mm double pointed needles and
CC yarn, cast on 36 (44: 52) sts.
Arrange the stitches evenly over four
needles and with the 5th needle, continue
as follows:
Round 1: * K1, p1; repeat from * to end
of round.
Change to MC yarn and continue to work
in k1, p1 rib in rounds as set until work
measures 4cm.
Change to a set of five 3.25mm needles.
Knit 3 rounds.
Round 1: K17 (21: 25), PM, M1L, k2,
M1R, PM, K17 (21: 25). *38 (46: 54) sts.*
Round 2: Knit.
Round 3: Knit to marker, SM, M1L, knit
to next marker, M1R, SM, knit to end of
round. *40 (48: 56) sts.*
Repeat the last two rounds a further 5
times. *50 (58: 66) sts.*
Next round: K18 (22: 26), place next
14 sts on stitch holder or length of spare
yarn, k to end of round.
Continue to knit the rem 36 (44: 50) sts on
needles until work measures 4 (4.5: 5) cm
from thumb separation.

Round 1: * K2, k2tog; repeat from * to end of round. *27 (33: 39) sts.*
Round 2: Knit.
Round 3: * K1, k2tog; repeat from * to end of round. *18 (22: 26) sts.*
Round 4: Knit.
Round 5: * K2tog; repeat from * to end of round. *9 (11: 13) sts.*
Round 6: *K2tog; repeat from * to last stitch, k1. *5 (6: 7) sts.*
Break yarn leaving a long tail, thread through rem sts and pull to close sts. Secure yarn on inside of mitten.
With 3.25mm needles, place 14 sts on stitch holder onto needles, mark round and join in new yarn.
Work 14 sts in round until work measures 2cm.
Round 1: * K2tog, k2; repeat from * to last 2 sts, k2tog. *10 sts.*
Round 2: * K2tog; repeat from * to end. *5 sts.*
Break yarn leaving a long tail, thread through rem sts and pull to close sts. Secure yarn on inside of mitten.

SNOWFLAKE CHART

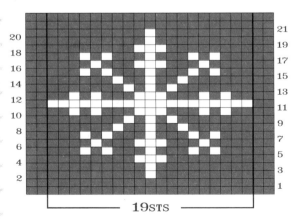

19sts

ADDING THE SNOWFLAKES

1 Thread a tapestry needle with the contrast yarn. On the centre of the palm of the left mitten, bring the needle through from the inside to the front six rows up from the rib cuff at the base of the stitch. Take the tapestry needle, from right to left, under the two loops of the stitch above the one being embroidered over.

2 Take the needle back through from the front to the inside at the base of the stitch where it originally came out to complete the embroidered stitch. Next, bring the needle through from the inside to the front again at the base of the stitch above.

3 Continue working in this way, using the Snowflake Chart as a reference, embroidering over the knitted stitches until the motif is completed. Repeat on the palm of right mitten.

MAKING THE CORD

Using 3.25mm double pointed needles and MC yarn, cast on 3 sts.
Knit the 3 sts.
Do not turn the work but slide the stitches to the other end of needle.
Bring the yarn round the back of the stitches and knit the 3 sts again.
Continue working in this way until the cord measures the desired length.
Sew the ends of the cord to the inside of each mitten just below the thumb.

MAKING THE POMPOMS

Following the instructions on page 49 and with the contrast colour yarn, make two pompoms approximately 3cm wide.
Sew the pompoms to the top of each mitten just above the rib cuff.

Tooth Fairy Pillow

110cm x 35cm white cotton sheeting
Air-erasable fabric pen
Large embroidery hoop
Stranded cotton embroidery threads
  in mid-brown, pink and ecru
12cm x 15cm pink cotton fabric
Matching sewing thread
1 button, 8mm in diameter
35cm length of pink ric rac
45cm x 30cm cushion pad
Basic sewing kit
Templates: Pocket and Boo
  embroidery (see page 132)

CUTTING OUT
from sheeting
  50cm x 32cm front panel
  55cm x 32cm back panel

from pink cotton
  two pockets (see page 132)

EMBROIDERING BOO

1 Using the template on page 132, transfer Boo's outline onto the bottom right corner of the front panel using an air-erasable fabric pen – see page 120.

2 Using the embroidery hoop to pull the fabric taut and two strands of ecru thread, fill in his tail, tummy, muzzle and outer eye with encroaching satin stitch. His inner ear is worked in the same way, with two strands of pink thread. Add a couple of short pink straight stitches to the outer eye and just above his nose.

3 Embroider Boo's whiskers in back stitch, with a single strand of brown thread, then use two strands to fill in his eye and to sew over the solid outline in stem stitch. Work small straight stitches around Boo's tail and the outside edge of his tummy, and over all the short lines. Finish off by working two tiny stitches in ecru to highlight his eye.

MAKING THE ENVELOPE

4 Tack the two pocket pieces together and, using matching thread, machine stitch 3mm in from the edges, leaving the short straight end open. Clip a small triangle from each corner so that when it is turned out it sits flat. Fold over and press a 5mm turning around each side.

5 Turn the pocket right side out and ease out the corners using a blunt pencil. Make a buttonhole loop at the pointed end – see page 121. Slip stitch the open straight edge closed. Fold the short straight edge up by 3.5cm, then overstitch the side edges to make a pocket. Sew the button to the front layer, in line with the buttonhole, and press down the flap.

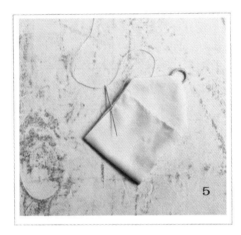

6 Pin the envelope to the front panel, just below Boo's outstretched paws. Sew it in place with small stitches, using matching sewing thread.

ADDING THE RIC RAC TRIM

7 Turn over 1cm from the left edge of the front panel and press, then turn over and press a second 4cm length. Slip the ric rac underneath the edge of this turning so that the scalloped edge peeps out from below the fold. Tack through all the layers to hold. Machine stitch 2mm from the edge of the fold.

ASSEMBLING THE PILLOWCASE

8 Make a 6mm single hem along one short side of the back panel piece. With right sides facing, line up and place the back over the front piece so that the hemmed edge of the back piece and the ric rac trimmed edge of the front piece are on the same side. Fold back the hemmed edge of the back panel to the same size as the front and pin the one short and two long raw edges together. Machine stitch around the three sides, leaving a 6mm seam allowance. Clip the corners on a diagonal, then neaten the seam with an overlocking or zigzag stitch. Turn the cover right side out and press flat.

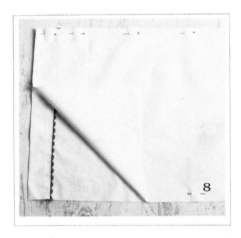

Hopscotch Mat

SAFETY FIRST: *Make sure you place this mat on a surface that will provide friction. Use it outside or on a carpet, do not use it on wooden floorboards as your child may slip.*

HEMMING THE MAT

1 Press back and stitch down a 15mm hem around all four edges of the brown fabric.

MARKING THE GRID

2 Draw two lines across the card to divide it into quarters. This will be your template for drawing up the eight rectangles.

3 Fold the mat in half lengthways to find the centre line and press lightly. Position the template landscape format, 8cm down from the short edge, so that the centre line of the card matches up with the crease. Draw around the edge of the card with a chalk pencil.

4 Reposition the template below and to the left of the chalk outline, so that the centre line of the card matches up with the left edge of the chalk outline above. Draw around the card once again, then move it to the right, so that the centre of the card lines up with the right edge of the first rectangle. Draw around the card again.

5 Using the placement guide below, outline five more rectangles to complete the grid.

ADDING THE TAPE

6 Use a glue stick to fix the tape outline in place before stitching. Cut eight horizontal lengths and fix along the chalk lines at the sides of the '3', '4', '5', '6' and '7' boxes.

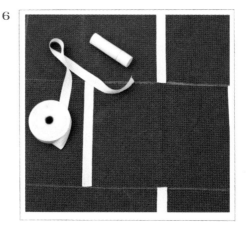

7 Now add a length of tape to fit around the top and side edges of the '8' box. Start at the bottom of one side of the box and take the piece of tape up, over the top and back down the other side. Fold the tape at a 45 degree angle at each corner, this will make a neat mitre. Frame the '1' and '2' boxes using a single piece of tape and using the same method as above. Start at one side. Fix down the sides of the '1' and '2' boxes and the bottom of the '1' box.

8 Cut a length of tape to fit along each of the four longer horizontal lines and stick them over the chalk marks and the raw ends of the other pieces of tape. Cut another length for the shorter horizontal line separating the '1' and '2' boxes.

9 Using matching cream sewing thread, stitch down each strip of tape using a 3mm-wide zigzag stitch.

MAKING THE NUMBERS

10 Trace the eight number templates on page 132 onto the paper side of the bonding web. Cut them out and iron each onto a range of different coloured fabrics following the manufacturer's instructions. Neatly cut around the pencil outline.

11 Peel off the backing paper of the bonding web and press the numbers onto their respective rectangles – double check against the placement guide to make sure that they are all in the right place. Zigzag stitch around the edge of each number using a thread that matches the fabric colour of the number.

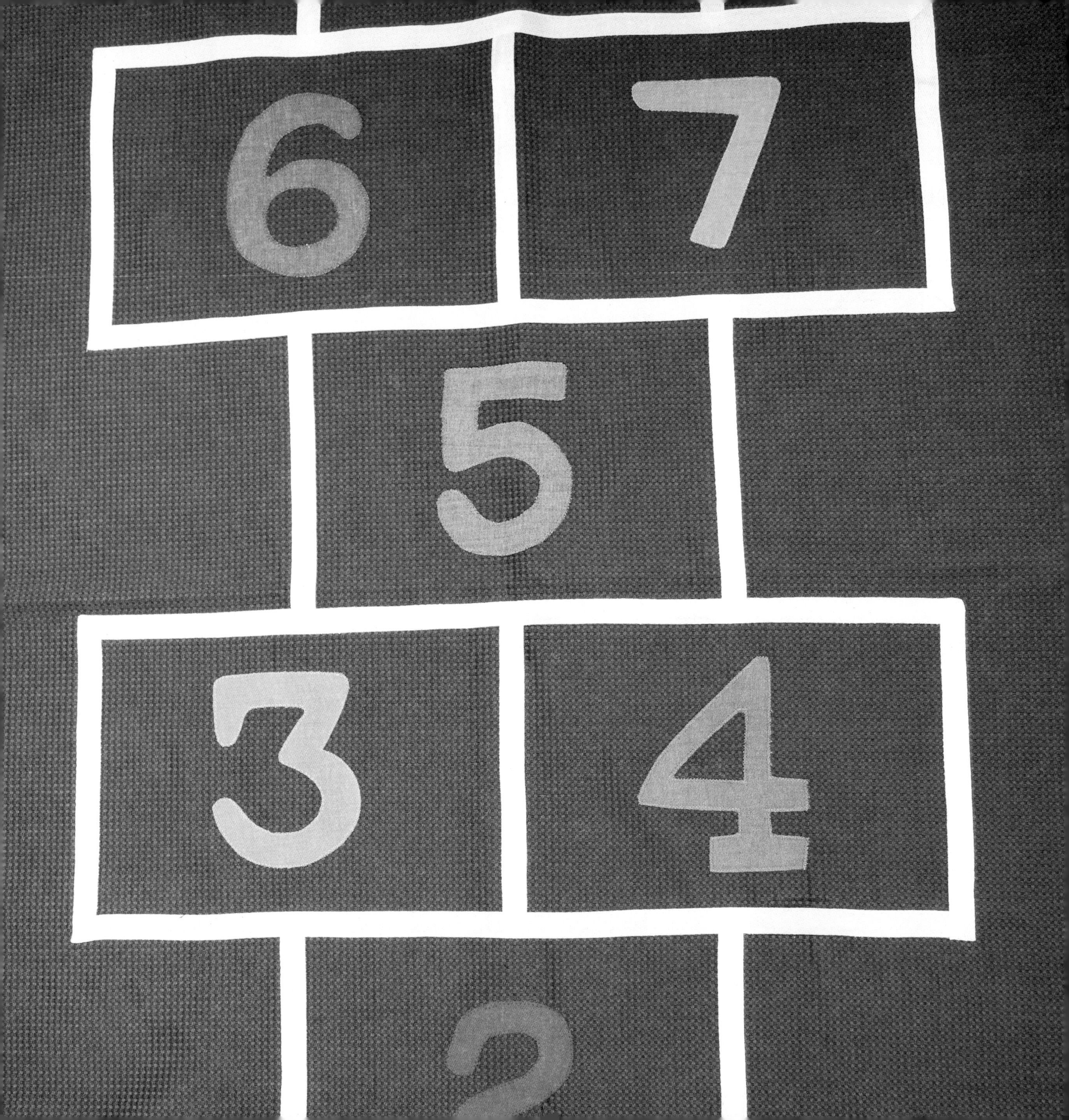

Explorer's Satchel

150cm x 60cm cotton poplin in 'Classic Belle & Boo' or 'Pirate Games' print (for the lining)
150cm x 60cm furnishing weight fabric
Roll of bias binding (for the edging)
10cm length of 2cm-wide tape
Five 2cm D-rings
Air-erasable fabric pen
1m of 2.5cm-wide webbing
Matching sewing thread
Basic sewing kit

Personalise your bag by choosing your favourite Belle & Boo fabric for the lining and vary the details - for example swap the binding for tape, or change the colours of the D-rings.

CUTTING OUT
from lining fabric
One 30cm x 30cm front
One 30cm x 30cm back
One 30cm x 30cm flap
Two 30cm x 10cm sides
One 30cm x 10cm base
One 30cm x 20cm inside pocket
Two 7cm x 12cm pocket flaps
Two 12cm x 13cm front pockets

from furnishing fabric
One 30cm x 30cm front
One 30cm x 30cm back
One 30cm x 30cm flap
Two 30cm x 10cm sides
One 30cm x 10cm base
One 30cm x 20cm large pocket
Two 7cm x 12cm pocket flaps
Two 12m x 13cm front pockets
Two 15cm x 10cm side pockets
One 5cm x 20cm zip pocket top
One 15cm x 20cm zip pocket front
One 20cm x 20cm zip pocket back
Two 2.5cm x 5cm tabs

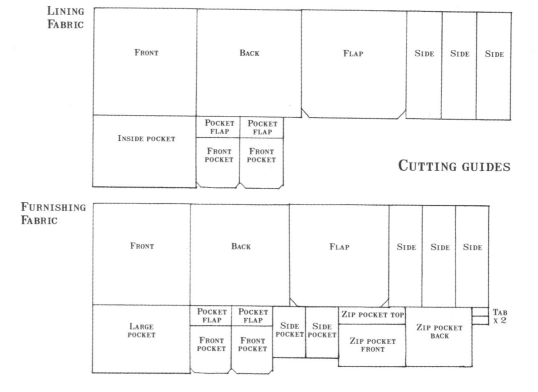

LINING FABRIC

| FRONT | BACK | FLAP | SIDE | SIDE | SIDE |

| INSIDE POCKET | POCKET FLAP | POCKET FLAP |
| | FRONT POCKET | FRONT POCKET |

CUTTING GUIDES

FURNISHING FABRIC

| FRONT | BACK | FLAP | SIDE | SIDE | SIDE |

| LARGE POCKET | POCKET FLAP | POCKET FLAP | SIDE POCKET | SIDE POCKET | ZIP POCKET TOP | ZIP POCKET BACK | TAB x 2 |
| | FRONT POCKET | FRONT POCKET | | | ZIP POCKET FRONT | | |

ASSEMBLING THE LARGE POCKET

1 Neaten the top edges of both main fabric front pockets with bias binding. Open out one side of the bias binding and stitch the raw edge of the binding along the raw top edge. Fold the binding over the edge to enclose and stitch in place. Fold back, press and tack down a 1cm turning along the other edges of the pockets.

2 To prepare both pocket flaps, fold a 2cm length of tape through a D-ring and tack the raw ends of the tape to the right side of the main fabric pocket flap at the centre of the bottom edge. With right sides facing, line up with the pocket flap lining and tack along the two short sides and bottom edge. Using the zip foot, machine stitch 6mm in from the edge, down the short sides and bottom, leaving the top edge open. Clip each corner on the diagonal and within 2mm of the stitch line and turn right side out.

3 Bias bind the top edge of the large pocket. Pin and tack the front pockets 3cm up from the bottom edge and 3cm in from the sides and machine stitch close to the folds. Work a few extra stitches at the top of the seams to reinforce the join.

4 With right sides facing, tack the top edge of the pocket flaps just above and in line with the top of the front pockets. Sew in place using a zigzag stitch to cover the raw edges. Fold the flaps over the top of the front pockets and press the seam flat. Tack the large pocket to the bag front.

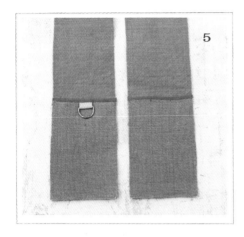

SEWING THE SIDES

5 Stitch a looped D-ring to the middle of the top edge of one side pocket as before. Bias bind the top edge of both side pockets, covering the raw edge of the D-ring loop. Using an air-erasable fabric pen, mark two lines on the other pocket, parallel to and 3.5cm in from the side edges. Leaving a 6mm seam allowance, stitch the sides and bottom of the pockets in line with the two bag sides, then stitch over the lines to make the pencil slots.

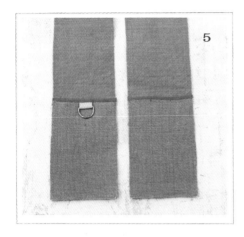

ASSEMBLING THE BAG

6 With right sides facing, tack the bottom edges of both side pieces to the short ends of the base. Machine stitch 1cm from the edge, sewing along one edge at a time and leaving 1cm unstitched at each end of both seams. With right sides facing, pin the front of the bag to both side pieces and a long side of the base. Stitch in place 1cm from the edge.

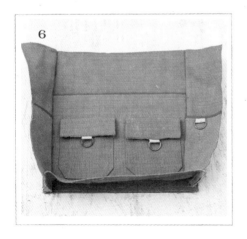

7 With right sides facing, sew the back piece to the open sides and the base in the same way as the front to complete the main bag. Diagonally clip the corners within 2mm of the stitch line, turn right side out and press lightly.

8 With right sides facing, pin and tack the flap lining to the flap, around both sides and the bottom edge. Leave the top open. Machine stitch, leaving a 1cm seam allowance around each edge, then diagonally clip the corners to within 2mm of the stitch line and turn right side out. With the right sides facing, pin the top edge centrally to the top edge of the bag back and sew the two together with a 6mm seam allowance.

MAKING UP THE LINING
9 Bias bind the top edge of the inside pocket, then press it in half widthways. Unfold the pocket and line it up and pin it to the bottom edge of the front lining piece. Machine stitch along the crease to divide the pocket in half.

10 Sew the top and bottom of the zip pocket front to either side of the zip to enclose. With right sides facing, line up and pin on the pocket back. Machine stitch both sides and the bottom edge, leaving the top open. Clip the corners and turn right side out. Sew the top edges together leaving a 6mm seam. Stitch the pocket centrally to the top edge of the back lining piece.

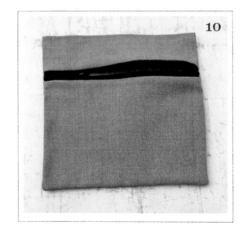

11 Assemble the lining in the same order and using the same method as the main bag (see steps 6–8), stitching 1cm seam allowances throughout.

PUTTING THE SATCHEL TOGETHER
12 Slip the lining inside the main bag so that the zip pocket is next to the flap at the back. Match up the seams, then tack all around the top edge to hold in place. Sew the two together, leaving a 1cm seam, then trim the seam allowance back to 5mm. Bias bind the top edges to neaten.

13 Securely stitch a D-ring onto each end of the webbing strap. Press back a 15mm seam along each side edge of both tabs. You can use a 10cm length of tape instead of the tabs if you wish. Thread a tab through a D-ring and stitch the folded raw ends to one side of the bag, on the inside edge. Join the other end of the strap to the other side of the inside of the bag in the same way.

Clubhouse Flag

70cm x 55cm black cotton
Fusible bonding web
40cm x 40cm white cotton
30cm x 20cm red cotton
Matching sewing thread
Four 2cm D-rings
Basic sewing kit
Templates: Skull, bones and
    initials (see pages 124 and 133)

PLACEMENT GUIDE

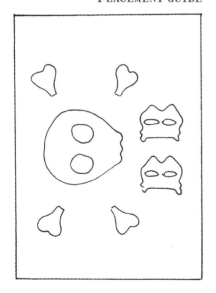

HEMMING THE FLAG

1 Press under 1cm of the raw edge around all four sides of the black cotton. Turn under a further 2cm all the way round and stitch in place to create a double hem.

ADDING THE APPLIQUÉ

2 Using the templates on page 133, trace the skull and four bones onto the paper side of your bonding web. Iron onto the white cotton following the manufacturer's instructions, then neatly cut out around the pencil outline.

3 Peel off the backing paper and arrange the skull and bones on the flag, leaving enough room at the bottom edge for the initials. Use the placement drawing on the left to help you with the layout.

4 Using the templates on page 124, photocopy and enlarge the chosen initials until they are a height of 10cm. Reverse the outlines, tracing them onto the paper side of the bonding web so that they appear to be backwards. Fuse the adhesive side onto the red cotton and cut out. Peel off the paper and position them below the skull. Iron in place.

5 Neaten the raw edges of the shapes by machine stitching in a 3mm satin stitch, using red thread for the edge of the letters and white for the skull and bones.

ADDING THE D-RINGS

6 From the remaining red cotton, cut a 28cm x 6cm strip. Fold it in half lengthways and pin the open long edge together. Machine stitch using matching thread, leaving a 6mm seam allowance. Turn the fabric right side out. Press flat so the seam lies at the back. Cut the strip into four 7cm lengths to make the tabs.

7 Thread a tab through a D-ring and fold the tab in half around the ring so that the seam lies inwards. Pin the ends to the wrong side of one of the corners of the flag and secure by sewing in place either by hand or machine. Repeat with the remaining tabs and D-rings.

Ballet Bag

CUTTING OUT

from 'Ava & Friends' cotton poplin
Two 35cm x 47cm rectangles
(for the outer bag)

from cream cotton
Two 35cm x 47cm rectangles
(for the lining)

SEAMS
The seam allowance throughout is 1cm.

FIXING THE D-RINGS
1 Thread one length of the 2.5cm-wide
tape through a D-ring and tack the two
ends together. Matching the raw edges,
sew the tape to the bottom corner of the
right side of one of the outer bag pieces,
2cm up from the bottom edge, with a 6mm
seam. Sew the other length of tape and
ring to the opposite bottom corner.

MARKING THE STITCH LINES
2 Fold over and press a 10cm turning
along the top edge of both outer bag
pieces. Unfold both pieces and fold over
and press a 7.5cm turning. You will now
have two folds, one 10cm from the top
and one 7.5cm from the top. These two
creases will act as a guide for stitching the
drawstring channel.

*Pick a sewing thread to match your
main fabric: we've used a contrasting
colour so that the seam lines clearly
show up in the photographs.*

STITCHING THE OUTER BAG

3 With right sides facing, pin the two outer bag pieces together. Sew along both sides and the bottom edge, leaving the 2.5cm gap between the creases along the two sides unstitched.

4 Clip a small triangle from the corners, to within 3mm of the stitch line, then fold back and press the seam allowances inwards on both sides of the bag.

SEWING THE LINING

5 Pin the two sides of the lining together and machine stitch both sides and the bottom edge. Leave a 10cm gap unstitched in the centre of the bottom edge. Trim the corners and press the seam allowances inwards as for the main bag (see step 4).

PUTTING THE BAG TOGETHER

6 Turn the outer bag right side out and slip it inside the lining. Line up the pieces and pin the side seams together. Machine stitch the two side seams together around the opening.

DOING THE TRICKY BIT

7 Now you will have to turn the whole thing right side out. Reach through the 10cm gap at the bottom of the lining and pull the outer bag all the way through. Ease out the corners of the lining, then stitch the two sides of the lining gap together by hand or machine. Push the lining back inside the outer bag.

STITCHING THE GATHERING CHANNEL

8 Work two rounds of stitching at the top of the bag, following along the crease lines pressed earlier and making sure you only sew through a single outer and lining layer at a time. You still want the top of the bag to be completely open. Top stitch around the opening to create a neat edge.

THREADING THE TIES

9 Cut the 15mm-wide length of tape in half widthways. Fasten a safety pin to one end of one strip. Feed the pin through the right side of the channel, out at the left and then back along the channel on the other side of the bag, bringing the tape out through the right opening again. Thread the two ends of the tape through the D-ring on the right side of the bag and stitch the ends securely together. Repeat this method with the second length of tape, starting at the left opening this time.

Quiet Book

40cm x 20cm oatmeal linen
20cm x 10cm orange cotton
90cm x 20cm white linen
40cm x 25cm green cotton
30cm x 10cm turquoise cotton
30cm length of cotton poplin in 'Classic
   Belle & Boo' print (137cm width)
20cm x 20cm cotton poplin in 'Pirate
   Games' print
15cm x 10cm pink spot print cotton
25cm x 5cm yellow spot print cotton

20cm length of 4mm-wide pink ribbon
20cm length of narrow white ric rac
25cm length of wide fawn ric rac
30cm length of 1cm-wide lace
30cm length of 3mm diameter brown cord

15cm x 10cm pink craft felt
20cm x 30cm light brown craft felt
10cm x 5cm orange craft felt
10cm x 5cm light blue craft felt
10cm x 5cm lilac craft felt
20cm x 10cm yellow craft felt
25cm x 10cm red craft felt
10cm x 10cm black craft felt

Stranded cotton embroidery thread in
   light green, yellow, gold, orange, lemon,
   pink, red, dark turquoise, white, lilac,
   dark brown and light brown

3 miniature clothes pegs
3 press studs
One 1cm diameter shank button
Sixteen 3cm diameter buttons
15cm zip
One 1cm-wide decorative button

Fusible bonding web
Scissors
Air-erasable fabric pen
Basic sewing kit

Templates: Numbers, house, trees, leaves,
   apron, Boo with strings, balloons,
   teepee and Boo finger puppet (see pages
   134–137)

TIP *Always use a scrap of cotton to protect the surface of the felt shapes when you are pressing them in place.*

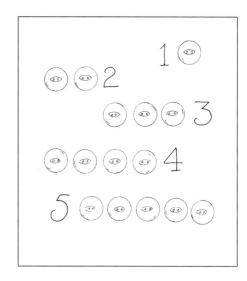

PLACEMENT GUIDES

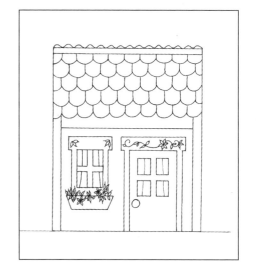

Numbers: page 1

Cutting out
from oatmeal linen
    One 20cm x 20cm square
from orange cotton
    One 20cm x 7cm strip

Making up the page
1 With right sides facing, line up a long side of the orange cotton with a raw edge of the linen. Pin in place, then machine stitch leaving a 6mm seam. Fold back and press the seam allowance open.

Embroidering the numbers
2 Following the placement guide on page 74, transfer the number outlines from page 134 and the button positions onto the front of the linen. Chain stitch over each number using three strands of thread, stitch '1' in orange, '2' in lemon, '3' in pink, '4' in white and '5' in lilac.

Adding the buttons
3 Sew the buttons securely in place in the marked positions, using thread to match.

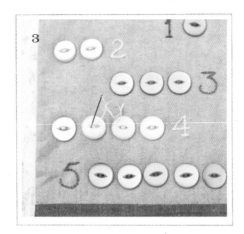

Wendy House: page 2

Cutting out
from white linen
    One 20cm x 20cm square
from green cotton
    One 20cm x 7cm strip
from turquoise cotton
    Two 2cm x 10cm strips

1 Make up the page from white linen and green cotton as for step 1 of Page 1.

Preparing the pieces
2 Using the templates on page 135, cut the door and window from black felt. Trace the other house shapes onto bonding web and cut out. Following the manufacturer's instructions, press the house front and main door onto red, the roof, coping and curtains onto pink and the door and window frames and box, door curtains and glazing onto yellow felt. Cut out.

3 Pick 2 images on the Classic fabric to fit the door and window. Add bonding web to the back. Press a narrow turning along the long edges of the turquoise strips.

Assembling the house
4 Follow the placement guide on page 74 for this stage. Position the images on the white linen, to fit behind the door and the window. Following the manufacturer's instructions, iron down the images, then press the house front over the top, lining up with the bottom of the white linen and images. Tack the turquoise strips along each side of the house. Press on the roof, leaving a gap of white at the top of the house front, but covering the ends of the turquoise strips. Place the ric rac along the top edge of the roof, then cover the bottom of the ric rac with the coping.

Making up the door & window
5 Press the door frame and window frame and box in place. Press the pink curtains to the edges of the window and top with glazing bars. Position the yellow curtains on the black door behind the bars of the red main door. Press the curtains then the main door in place. Blanket stitch around the inside of the window and window box in pink and the door in red. Stitch a button door knob to the red front door.

FINISHING OFF

6 Sew the door in place along the right edge. Stitch the window in place on the left-hand side. Using an air-erasable fabric pen, mark the tiles on the roof and back stitch along the lines using two strands of dark turquoise thread. Add the flowers and leaves to the window box and then embroider the lintels.

WASH DAY: PAGES 3 AND 4

CUTTING OUT
from white linen
  One 38cm x 20cm rectangle
from green cotton
  One 38cm x 7cm strip
from pink spot print cotton
  2 aprons
from yellow spot print cotton
  One 15cm x 5cm strip (for skirt)
  One 5cm x 3.5cm rectangle (for bib)
from 'Classic Belle & Boo' cotton
  One 12cm x 12cm square

1 Make up the page from white linen and green cotton as for step 1 of Page 1.

MAKING THE TREES
2 Using the templates on page 136, trace the two trees onto bonding web. Cut out roughly. Following the manufacturer's instructions, press onto light brown felt and cut out. Iron tree 1 onto the edge of the left page and tree 2 onto the right.

ADDING THE POCKET
3 Press under and stitch down a 2cm hem along the top edge of the Classic fabric. Press a 1cm turning along the sides and the bottom edge. Tack the sides and the bottom of the pocket next to tree 2, so that the bottom edge lies along the top of the green cotton and the right side lies against the side of the tree. Stitch in place.

EMBROIDERING THE LEAVES
4 Using an air-erasable pen, transfer the leaf outlines onto the white fabric. Scatter five across the sky and add two oak leaves to the top right branch of tree 2. Embroider them with satin stitch, using three strands of orange or brown thread.

MAKING THE CLOTHES
5 Pin the two aprons together with right sides facing and machine stitch 3mm from the edge, leaving the neck open. Turn the fabric right side out through the gap. Press. Turn in the raw edges at the neck and tuck the ends of a 6cm length of pink ribbon into the corners to create a loop at the neck. Slip stitch the opening closed. Cut the remaining pink ribbon in half. Stitch an end of each length to the back of the apron, one on each side. These will act as the ties. Using the template on page 136, cut the pocket from pink felt and slip stitch to the front of the apron.

6 For the dress, stitch together the short ends of the yellow strip. Press a 6mm turning around the top and bottom edges. Sew a length of lace to the bottom edge, turn the skirt right side out and press so that the join is at the back. Starting at one edge of the join, stitch around the top of the skirt and pull the ends of the thread together to gather the waist and tie off. Fold the bib in half lengthways and stitch the side edges. Turn right side out and press the join to the back. Cut two 8cm lengths of lace and sew one to each side of the bottom of the front of the bib at a slight outward angle. Cross over at the back and sew to the back of the skirt.

BOO AND BALLOONS: PAGE 5

CUTTING OUT
from white linen
     One 20cm x 20cm square
from green cotton
     One 20cm x 7cm strip
from coloured felt
     2 balloons from each chosen colour

1 Make up the page from white linen and green cotton as for step 1 of Page 1.

EMBROIDERING THE OUTLINES
2 Using an air-erasable pen, transfer the Boo, string and stud outlines from page 137 onto the left side of the page, with Boo sitting on the edge of the green cotton. Using two strands of dark brown thread, embroider Boo in stem stitch. Back stitch along the balloon strings in lilac, blue and orange.

3 Sew the recessed halves of the three press studs in place. Sew the other halves to a balloon of each colour.

MAKING UP THE BALLOONS
4 Pin the two sides of each matching balloon together (making sure that the press stud side is right side out) and sew a round of blanket stitch around the outside edge using two strands of matching embroidery thread.

5 Finish off by working a few yellow and white lazy daisies and French knots over the green cotton 'lawn'.

TEEPEE: PAGE 6

CUTTING OUT
from oatmeal linen
     One 20cm x 20cm square
from turquoise cotton
     One 20cm x 7cm strip
     1 teepee point
from 'Pirate Games' cotton
     2 teepees, 1 reversed
from light brown felt
     2 Boo finger puppets, 1 reversed

1 Make the page from oatmeal linen and turquoise cotton as for step 1 of Page 1.

STITCHING THE TEEPEE

2 Press a 6mm turning along the diagonal and long straight edges of both teepees. Position the zip between the two straight edges, so that the front of the zip is facing out from between the right sides of the fabric. Tack down and stitch in place.

3 Tack the teepee to the middle of the page so that it lines up with the edge of the turquoise fabric. Sew in place along all 3 sides, leaving a 3mm seam allowance. Pin, then stitch the ric rac along the bottom edge of the teepee, turning under the two ends neatly. Press under the edges of the turquoise teepee point and sew it in place at the top of the page. Conceal the join with another short length of ric rac.

MAKING THE FINGER PUPPET

4 Using the template on page 137, trace Boo's ears and tummy onto bonding web. Press onto pink felt, then cut out and fuse in place on one of the puppet shapes. Embroider his features with dark brown thread. Pin the other felt puppet to the wrong side of the first and sew together (leaving the bottom open) using blanket stitch. Zip Boo safely into the teepee.

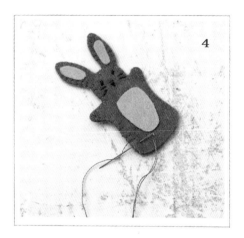

ASSEMBLING THE BOOK

CUTTING OUT
from 'Classic Belle & Boo' cotton
One 38cm x 27cm rectangle

1 With right sides facing, pin the left edge of page 6 to the right edge of page 1. Sew a 1cm seam along this edge, leaving 5cm of fabric unstitched at one end. Press back the seam allowance.

2 With right sides facing, line up and pin the pages to the cover and sew around the outside, with a 1cm seam allowance. Clip the corners on the diagonal. Using the gap left between the pages, pull the fabric right side out. Push out the corners and press. Slip stitch the gap closed.

3 Join pages 2 and 5 as for step 1. Join these pages to the double page 3 and 4 as for step 2. Line up and pin the two layers together, so that pages 1 and 6 face pages 2 and 5. The pages of the booklet should now be in order, with the cover on the outside. Sew the booklet together along the spine. Finish off by sewing the ends of the brown cord to the top branches of the two trees on the centre page. Use miniature clothes pegs to pin the apron and dress to this washing line.

Kite Rewards Chart

Sheet of A3 foamboard
Selection of coloured papers in
    plains and prints
Sharp pencil
Craft knife or scissors
Metal ruler
Length of jute string
Clear adhesive or spray
    fixative
Selection of coloured ribbons
    in plains and ginghams
Template: Kite (see page 139)

PREPARING THE KITE BASE

1 Using a photocopier, enlarge the kite template on page 139 to your chosen size. For example, for an A4-sized kite you will need to enlarge the template by 350%. Cut out the kite shape carefully, position it centrally on the foamboard and lightly draw around the outside edge with a sharp pencil. Using a craft knife and metal ruler, cut the shape from the foamboard. Cut the enlarged template into four sections along the marked lines. This now gives you the templates needed to cut out the colours for your chosen quarters.

COVERING THE KITE BASE

2 Place the kite base onto the paper you have chosen for the main background. Lightly draw around the outside edge with a sharp pencil then cut carefully just inside the outline. Using clear adhesive or spray fixative, fix the coloured paper to the foamboard, lining up all the edges.

3 Using the prepared templates for the separate quarters, trace and cut your chosen shapes from the selection of coloured plain or print papers. Fix the cut-out quarters to the kite base in their respective positions.

ADDING THE KITE TAIL

4 Cut a length of string approximately twice the height of the kite base and, using clear adhesive, fix one end of the string to the reverse side of the kite base.

REWARDING WITH RIBBONS

5 Keep a selection of coloured ribbons to hand. Every time an action deserves rewarding, cut a 20cm length of ribbon to tie onto the kite tail in a neat bow.

Camera Bag

30cm x 20cm dark blue craft felt
15cm x 10cm dark grey craft felt
30cm x 20cm light grey craft felt
8cm x 6cm pale blue craft felt
Fusible bonding web
Dark blue, mid-grey, light grey
   and white stranded cotton
   embroidery thread
3cm diameter button
1cm press stud
Small (about 1cm diameter)
   red and grey buttons
15cm red nylon zip
80cm length of 1cm-wide
   black ribbon
15cm x 2cm strip of thin card
Templates: Camera outline
   (with slot), camera front,
   small circle with lines, large
   circle, view finder, film
   winder (see page 138)

CUTTING OUT
from bonding web
Trace and roughly cut out 2 cameras (one reversed with a slot), 1 camera front, 1 large circle, 2 small circles, 1 view finder and 1 film winder from the bonding web.

Following the manufacturer's instructions, fuse both camera pieces and 1 small circle onto the dark blue felt. Fuse the camera front to the dark grey, the large circle and film winder to the light grey and the second small circle and the view finder to the pale blue felt. Cut out all the pieces following the pencil outlines.

from light grey felt
Two 12 x 8cm rectangles
(for the lining)

ASSEMBLING THE FRONT
1 Peel the backing paper off every piece apart from the two cameras. Using a scrap of cotton fabric to protect the felt and following the manufacturer's instructions, press the camera front to one of the main camera pieces, then add the three circles, view finder and film winder following the placement guide shown on the left.

EMBROIDERING THE OUTLINES
2 Remove the paper from the back of the front camera piece. Each of the pieces is edged in blanket stitch, worked with three strands of thread – see how to do this on page 121. The large circle is outlined in dark blue thread and the small circle in a pale grey. The inside edges of the camera front (where they overlap the main camera) are stitched in a mid-grey.

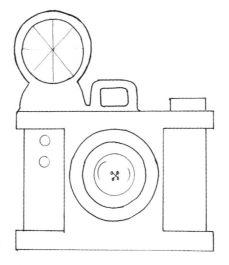

PLACEMENT GUIDE

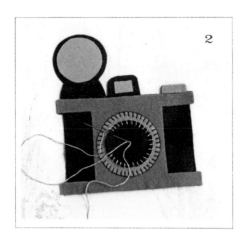

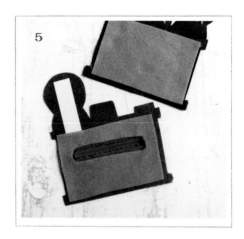

ADDING THE ZIP

4 Cut out the shaded slot from the second camera piece according to the template on page 138 and peel off the backing. Trim the end off the zip so that it fits neatly inside of the slot. Place the zip so that the front of the zip is visible through the right side of the back camera piece. Pin it in place and oversew the felt to the zip tape.

3 Lightly mark the lines that cross the small pale blue circle with a pencil and ruler according to the guide on page 84, then embroider over them in back stitch using three strands of white thread. Work a round of pale blue blanket stitch around the outside edge, then outline the view finder in the same colour.

PUTTING THE BAG TOGETHER

6 With wrong sides facing, place the front and back pieces together, matching up the outside edges as closely as possible. Place a cotton cloth over the camera and gently press to fuse the two pieces. Now trim the edges so that they are lined up exactly.

7 As before, work dark blue blanket stitch around the outside of the flash gun, view finder and the dark blue short sides of the camera. The top, bottom and dark grey side edges of the camera front are outlined in mid-grey and the film winder in white.

8 Sew the base of the press stud to the centre of the flash, then add the two small buttons to the left side of the camera and the large button to the centre of the lens.

9 Securely sew the two ends of the ribbon to the top corners of the camera back to make the strap.

LINING THE BAG

5 Glue the card strip over the wrong side of the flash gun on the back camera piece. This will keep the flash upright. Cut a slot from a lining piece to match up with the size of the zip. Gently press both lining pieces into position on the wrong side of the front and back camera pieces, using the tip of the iron for precision.

Pullalong Elephant

60cm x 50cm brown cotton
Clear ruler
Air-erasable fabric pen
Safety standard toy stuffing
Two 6mm toy safety eyes or
    buttons
50cm length of cotton string
Length of spot print ribbon
Matching sewing thread
Basic sewing kit
Templates: Body, head gusset,
    underbody and ears (see
    page 139)

for the trolley
4 long nails with flat heads
Four 3cm toy wheels or wood
    discs with central holes
Wood glue
2 lengths of wood, each 6cm x
    1.5cm x 1.5cm (for the axles)
2 lengths of wood, each 6cm x
    1.5cm x 1.2cm
Rectangle of wood, 6cm x
    20cm x 1.2cm
1 small screw eye
1m of string
Glue gun

CUTTING OUT
Follow the broken line across the body pattern when cutting out the underbody.

from the brown cotton
    2 bodies, 1 reversed
    1 head gusset
    2 underbodies, 1 reversed
    4 ears, 2 reversed

MARKING UP
the body
    Transfer the dart lines and points
    A & B
    Mark the eye and ear positions

the ears
    Mark both ends of the gathering line

SEAMS
The seam allowance is 6mm throughout. Mark the stitch line on each piece, 6mm from the edge, using a ruler and an air-erasable fabric pen.

Reinforce both ends of each seam with two or three stitches worked in the reverse direction.

CUTTING GUIDE

Our elephant is stitched in a contrasting thread so that the seam lines are clear, but you should use a thread that matches your fabric.

ADDING THE DARTS

1 Fold one of the body pieces so that the two edges of the dart are lined up, with right sides facing. Sew all the way along the marked line. Do the same on the other body piece.

ADDING THE HEAD GUSSET

2 With right sides facing, pin the head gusset to one of the bodies. Match points A and B on the gusset seam line with points A and B marked on the top of the elephant's head as shown on page 139. Tack and then machine stitch, leaving the seam allowance at each end of the gusset piece unstitched.

JOINING THE UNDERBODY

3 With right sides facing, pin and tack the two underbodies together along the top edge. Sew along the marked line, leaving the seam allowance open at each end.

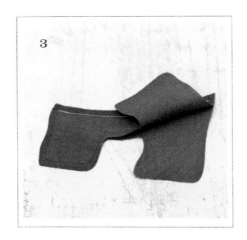

4 Open out the underbody. With right sides facing, pin one side of the underbody to the corresponding body piece. Tack together around the outside edge of the underbody piece. Machine stitch, once again leaving the 6mm seam allowance unstitched at each end.

ADDING THE OTHER SIDE OF THE BODY

5 With right sides facing, pin on the second body. Firstly pin together where points A and B are marked on the head gusset, pin the trunk and line up the two darts. Carefully match and pin together the legs, then tack the outside edges together, again leaving the seam allowances free.

6 Machine stitch along the seam in three sections. Start by opening out the underbelly and stitch the loose underbelly to the corresponding legs of the second body piece. Continue to stitch around each leg following the seam line, working from head to tail. Leave the seam allowances unstitched.

7 For the second section, turn the elephant over and sew along the open side of the gusset from B to A. Stitch over the seam allowance at A, continuing around the head and trunk and ending at the underbelly seam. There should now only be a gap along the back of the elephant, this final section will be stitched closed once the elephant is stuffed.

8 Now trim the allowance so that the seams will open out once turned right side out. Take care to cut no more than 3mm from the stitch line. Cut a small triangle of fabric from the corners of the feet and trunk. Make small snips into each of the curved seams at 1cm intervals and notch the right angles. Press back the seam allowance on either side of the opening at the elephant's back.

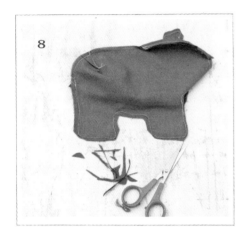

STUFFING THE ELEPHANT

9 Reach through the gap at the back and pull the fabric right the way through, turning the elephant right side out. Gently ease out the seams and corners with a knitting needle. Start by filling the trunk with small clumps of toy stuffing. Use the knitting needle to push the stuffing right to the tip of the trunk and keep packing it down. Next, firmly stuff the legs, then the head and body.

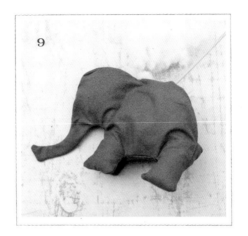

10 Close the gap along the back of the elephant using a slip stitch.

MAKING THE EARS

11 Pin the ears together in pairs with right sides facing. Machine stitch 4mm from the edge leaving a 2–3cm gap at the centre of the top edge. Press back the seam allowance either side of the opening. Clip away the corners and around the curves and turn right side out.

12 Sew a line of small running stitches between the two gathering points marked on page 139, and draw the threads up so that the gathering points are about 3cm apart, the ears have a dome shape and the gap is closed. Pin the ears to the head on either side of the gusset along the stitch line and where indicated on page 139 with the slightly shorter edge of the ear to the front. Sew securely in place.

FINISHING OFF

13 Firmly sew the eyes in place at the marked spots on either side of the elephant's head. Tie a length of ribbon around the neck and finish with a bow.

14 To make the tail, cut three 20cm lengths of string and knot them together at one end. Plait the three strands for 8cm and finish with a knot. Trim off the excess string from both ends, leaving a 2cm tassel at one end and trimming close to the knot at the other. Carefully use the point of your scissors to make a small hole next to the back seam of the elephant, about 3cm down from the darts. Push the close cut knot through the gap and stitch in place.

MAKING THE TROLLEY

15 Nail a wheel to each end of the two 1.5cm x 1.5cm wooden axles. Glue the two 6cm x 1.5cm x 1.2cm lengths of wood flush against the short ends of the large wooden rectangle base, then glue the axles next to them, underneath the base. When dry, sand lightly and paint if you like. Fix the screw eye to the middle of one end of the base and tie on the string. Use a glue gun to fix the soles of the elephant's feet to the top of the trolley.

TROLLEY: We used the base of an old wooden truck to make the pullalong base for the elephant, but you can follow the instructions on the left to make a similar one. Alternatively, look in the toy box for an old toy which can be upcycled and repainted.

SAFETY FIRST: This is a toy for a toddler. If this is being given to a younger child do not sew on eyes, but instead mark with fabric pens. Also make sure the ears are securely sewn in place and won't come off as these are small parts that may look tempting to try to swallow! Finally, make sure you are there to supervise whilst the child is playing as the string may tangle.

Lollipop Soaps

YOU WILL NEED

Clear melt-and-pour soap base
(you will need approximately
50g per lollipop soap)
Microwave-safe jug
Small amount of surgical spirit
in a spritzer bottle
Liquid soap dye in your
chosen colours
Fragrance oils in your
chosen scent
Plastic lollipop mould (with
cover)
Wooden lollipop sticks
Bulldog clips
Short lengths of ribbon
Small, clear plastic
presentation bags

MELTING THE SOAP BASE
1 Cut the soap base into chunks and
place in a microwave-safe jug. Heat in
a microwave on medium power for 30
seconds. Stir to check the chunks have
just melted and, if necessary, heat for
a further 30 seconds. Do not allow the
soap to boil. Remove the jug from the
microwave and spritz the melted soap
with the surgical spirit to remove any
air bubbles from the surface.

NOTE: *Once you have used the lollipop
mould for making these soaps, it is not
advisable to use it for making edible ice
lollies as the soap and fragrance oils
may leave an aftertaste.*

ADDING THE COLOUR AND FRAGRANCE
2 Add one or two drops of your chosen
dye. Stir to check the colour and, if
necessary, add more drops to strengthen
the shade. Add a few drops of fragrance
oil. Stir to check the scent, adding a few
more drops for a stronger scent. Stir in
any other additional ingredients, such
as poppy seeds, at this point. Spritz the
soap's surface again with the surgical
spirit, until no air bubbles are visible.

VARIATION: *You can also add poppy
seeds or oatmeal for exfoliation, or
some lavender flowers to release a hit
of extra fragrance.*

MOULDING THE LOLLIPOP SOAPS

3 Carefully pour the liquid soap into the lollipop mould. Spritz the surface again until no air bubbles are visible.

ADDING THE LOLLIPOP STICKS

4 Working quickly before the soap sets, place the cover over the mould. Place a bulldog clip one-third of the way down a wooden lollipop stick (this will ensure that the stick does not sink to the bottom of the mould). Place the cover over the mould, guiding the lollipop stick through the slot in the cover. Leave the soap to set for at least 60 minutes.

DEMOULDING THE LOLLIPOP SOAPS

5 Once set, remove the bulldog clips from the lollipop sticks and carefully lift off the cover. Gently tap the stick. If it moves, the soap is not fully set so leave it a little longer to fully harden.

6 Squeeze all the way round the mould until the soap comes away from the sides. Slide the soap from the mould by holding onto the lollipop stick. Allow the soaps to air-dry for at least 5 minutes.

PRESENTING THE LOLLIPOP SOAPS

7 Slide the soap in a presentation bag. Tie a short length of ribbon around the bottom of the lollipop stick to seal the bag.

Friendship Bracelets

for the plaited bracelet
Stranded cotton embroidery
thread in cerise, pink
and lime

for the beaded bracelet
Stranded cotton embroidery
thread in pink and cerise
Approximately 20 small beads
with large centre holes

for the woven bracelet
Stranded cotton embroidery
thread in pink, cerise, lime
and blue

NOTE: *To make sure the instructions are clear, we have used a much thicker thread in the photographs than the stranded cotton embroidery thread you will be using.*

MAKING THE PLAITED BRACELET

1 Cut a 60cm length from each colour of the embroidery thread. Knot the threads tightly together at one end, and trim the thread above the knot to make even. Pin the knot to a cushion or the arm of an upholstered chair. Arrange the threads in the following order, left to right: cerise, pink, lime.

2 A simple three-strand plait is made by moving the threads, alternatively from the left and then the right into the centre. Start by passing the cerise thread over the top of the pink thread.

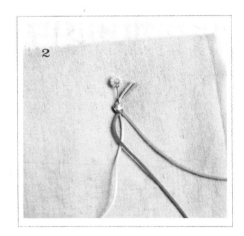

3 Now pass the green thread on the right over the cerise thread, so that it now lies in the centre.

4 Pass the pink thread over the green thread, moving the pink thread to the centre. Carry on moving the threads from the left and right alternately into the centre until the bracelet is one and a half times the length of your child's wrist. Knot the threads together to hold the plait in place and trim away any excess.

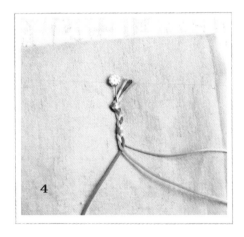

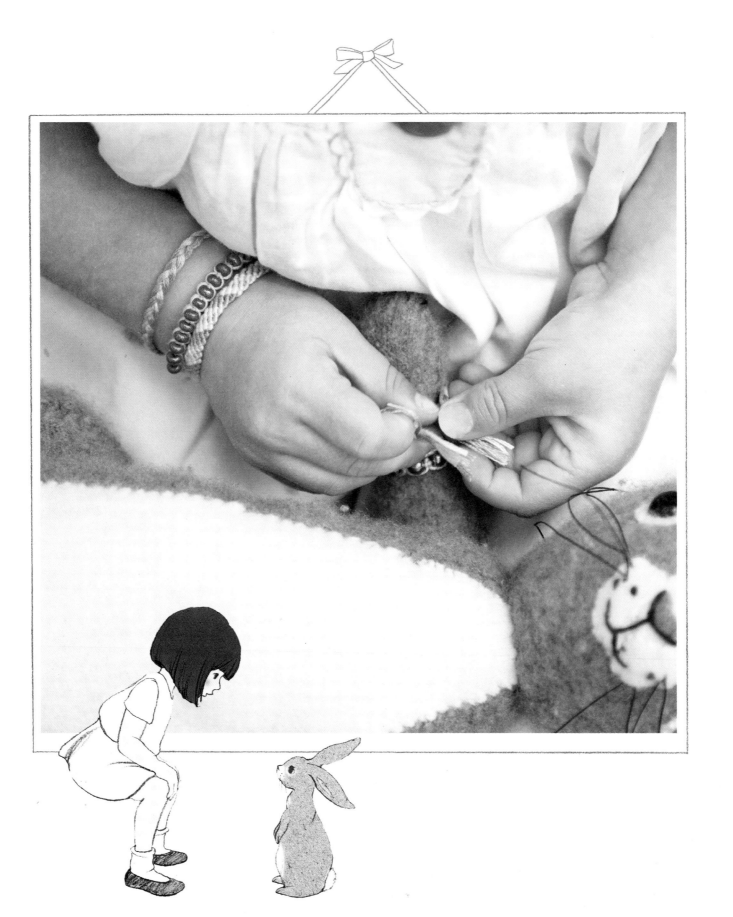

MAKING THE BEADED BRACELET

1 Cut two 70cm lengths of cerise thread and a 30cm length of pink thread. Knot the ends together and trim. Following the steps on page 98, make a 5cm plait, ending with the pink thread in the centre. Pin down the end of the plait to hold in place. Thread all the beads onto the pink thread.

2 The plait is secured by making a flat double knot using the two cerise threads. To make the first half of the double knot, take the right cerise thread behind the pink and up over the left cerise thread.

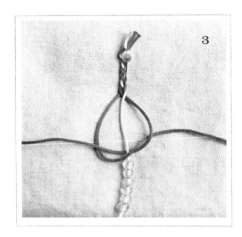

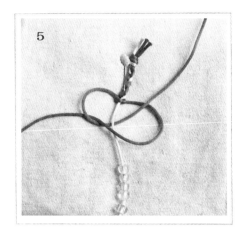

4 Repeat to make a second knot and pull until tight.

6 Continue knotting on more of the beads until the bracelet just fits around your child's wrist. Finish off with another 5cm plait, then tie off the open ends and trim away the excess thread.

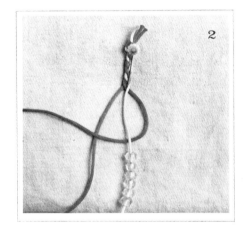

3 Take the bottom of the left thread (keeping the right thread over the top) over the pink thread and through and under the right thread. Pull the ends gently upwards to tie.

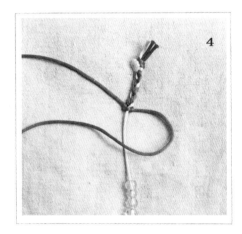

5 Make another looped knot, but do not pull tight. Slide one of the beads up the pink centre thread, then pull the knot tight below it. Make another knot below it to hold in place.

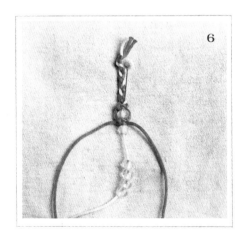

MAKING THE WOVEN BRACELET

1 This woven bracelet can be made in any width you like by simply adding more threads. Cut four 70cm lengths of embroidery thread, one from each colour. Knot them together 10cm from one end. Pin the knot to a cushion or the arm of an upholstered chair. Arrange them in the following order from left to right: cerise, lime, blue and pink. You will need to work from left to right throughout this process.

2 Make a flat double knot. Pass the cerise thread over the top and then back behind the lime thread. Lay the end over the top of the cerise thread.

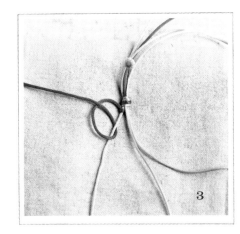

4 Now use the cerise thread to make the same double knot over the blue thread.

5 Complete the row, by making a double knot with the cerise thread over the pink. The cerise thread now sits on the right.

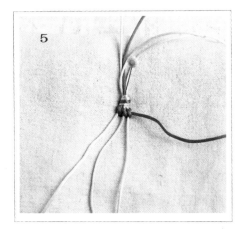

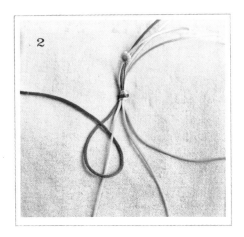

3 Pull the cerise thread up to the left, so that the loop moves to the top of the lime thread. Repeat this action with the cerise thread to form a double knot.

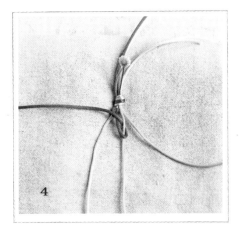

6 Weave the next row from left to right using the lime thread. Continue working in this way, alternating the colours, until the bracelet is one and a half times the length of your child's wrist. Tie the threads together and trim the ends.

Meadow Picnic Blanket

Large dark green blanket or throw
4ply mercerised cotton yarn, such
  as Yeoman's Cotton Cannele
MC   1 x 100g ball in yellow
CC   1 x 100g ball in white
2.5mm crochet hook
Large-eyed needle

ABBREVIATIONS

ch   chain
dc   double crochet
dtr   double treble
htr   half treble
sl st   slip stitch
sp   space
tr   treble

DAISY

MAKING A FOUNDATION RING

1 With MC yarn and 2.5mm hook, make
5ch, join with sl st to 1st ch to make a ring.

WORKING THE DAISY CENTRE

2 Work 2ch, 11htr into ring, sl st to 2nd
ch. Fasten off leaving a short tail of yarn.

WORKING THE DAISY PETALS

3 Join CC yarn to top of 1st htr. Work
3ch, 3tr into same stitch. Remove hook
from loop and reinsert in 3rd ch, then
place back through loop. Pull yarn
through loop and work 2ch. * Work 4tr
into next htr, remove hook from loop and
reinsert in top of 1st tr, then place back
through loop. Pull yarn through ch st (this
makes 1 popcorn stitch petal). Work 2ch.

Repeat from * to end of round to make
a further 11 petals. Sl st into 1st 2ch sp.
Fasten off leaving a 25cm tail of yarn.
Weave in the MC yarn tail.

Vary the size of the daisies by working
9htr into the foundation ring to make a
smaller flower with fewer petals or by
working dtr instead of tr to make longer
petals for a larger flower.

BUTTERCUP

This is worked over a 'magic circle' foundation loop, which is drawn up once the flower is complete.

MAKING A MAGIC CIRCLE

4 Loop the MC yarn from right to left, then use the crochet hook to draw the working yarn through the loop from front to back. Pull the yarn tail so that the loop is 2–3cm in diameter.

WORKING THE BUTTERCUP PETALS

5 Supporting the loop with your thumb and finger, * work 2ch, 4dtr into magic circle, 1ch, 1dc into magic circle and over the tail of yarn (this makes 1 petal).

Repeat from * 3 times to work a further 4 petals. Fasten off leaving a 25cm tail of yarn.

Holding the flower, gently draw up the tail from the magic circle as tightly as possible. Knot the two ends together.

STITCHING THE FLOWERS TO THE BLANKET

6 Thread the yarn through a large-eyed needle and sew each flower securely to the blanket, working the stitches between the petals to keep a three-dimensional look. Scatter them randomly across the whole surface for a naturalistic look.

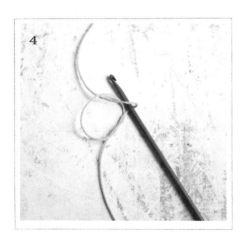

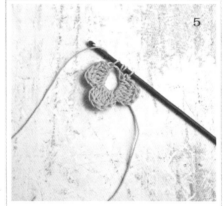

Snowflake Tree Wall Motif

YOU WILL NEED

Sheets of thin plain white
   paper (acid-free paper if
   possible as it will not turn
   yellow with age) or pre-cut
   quilling paper
Craft knife or scissors
Quilling tool
Clear adhesive
Wooden toothpick or cocktail
   stick
Dressmaker's pins
Sheet of foamboard
Template: Snowflake grid (see
   page 140)

CUTTING OUT
Cut the thin plain white paper into long narrow strips, approximately 5mm wide.

PREPARING THE TEMPLATE
Copy the snowflake grid template from page 140. Tape it to a sheet of foamboard.

MAKING THE SNOWFLAKE FRAMEWORK
1 From the narrow strips of paper, cut six 10cm lengths. Fold each of these six in half widthways. Crease the last 1cm of each free end inwards to create a 'wishbone' shape. Place these together, with the Vs pointing inwards, on the grid to form a circle. Using dabs of adhesive on a stick, join together the shapes where they touch. Using dressmaker's pins pushed into the foamboard, anchor the shapes in place until the adhesive is dry.

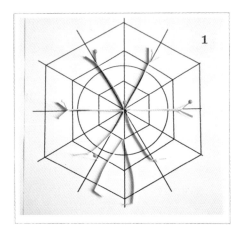

MAKING THE DECORATIVE SHAPES
2 Decide what shapes you want to use within the snowflake framework. Whatever shapes you choose, you need to make them in multiples of six. To make a set of simple 'teardrop' or 'leaf' shapes, cut 6, 12 or 18 narrow strips of paper all to the same length. Place the end of one in the slot at the end of the quilling tool and twist to wind into a spiral. Using dabs of adhesive, join the free end of the paper strip to the spiral to secure. To make a 'teardrop' shape, pinch one side of the circle. To make a 'leaf', pinch both sides.

FILLING IN THE SNOWFLAKE FRAMEWORK
3 Place your quilled shapes within the segments of the snowflake framework, creating a symmetrical pattern. Using dabs of adhesive, join together the quilled shapes and framework where they touch.

4 Add further rounds of quilled shapes to each segment of the snowflake until happy with your design. Experiment with a variety of shapes; as no two snowflakes are the same, you can indulge your imagination. Some of the more popular quilled shapes include the S scroll, V scroll, C scroll and the heart scroll.

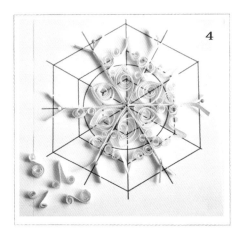

TO DISPLAY THE SNOWFLAKES
5 We cut a large tree silhouette from a roll of wallpaper and mounted it on a blank wall. We then cut and added small circles of pale and bright pink paper to the branches. Finally we added quilled snowflakes of varying sizes and designs to the branches of the tree. Alternatively, add loops of fine or invisible thread to one segment of each to create a hanging loop.

Patchwork Bedcover

YOU WILL NEED

Selection of lightweight cottons
in different colours and prints,
recycled from outgrown children's
clothing that has been laundered
and pressed
1m lightweight cream cotton
(136cm wide)
1.65m lightweight brown gingham
(136cm wide), for border
1m cotton poplin in 'Boo' print
(137cm wide), for backing
108cm x 140cm lightweight cotton
or bamboo quilt wadding, for
filling
3.8m brown ric rac trim
Recycled paper, such as old
envelopes, for backing paper
Matching and contrasting sewing
thread
Basic sewing kit
Templates: Hexagons (see page 140)

CUTTING OUT

Trace the hexagons from page 140 onto
thin cardboard, then cut out. Draw
around the small template onto recycled
paper, making enough backing papers for
each fabric hexagon. A throw for a child's
single bed will need 373 hexagons. Using
an air-erasable pen, draw around the large
template onto the wrong side of the fabric
and cut out.

from coloured cottons
205 large hexagons, in sets of 6 (plus
1 extra) from each print (for flowers)

from cream cotton
168 large hexagons (for background)

from brown gingham
Four 24.5cm x 146cm (for the border)
Four 24.5cm x 127cm (for the border)

from 'Boo' print cotton poplin
81cm x 100cm (for the backing)

PREPARING THE HEXAGON PATCHES

1 Take a backing paper hexagon and
place it centrally against the wrong side
of a fabric hexagon. Fold back each edge
of the fabric, fingerpressing as you work
around to create neat corners, and tack
down one side at a time by passing the
needle through the backing paper. Press.
Each 'flower' is made up of six 'petals'
around a centre, so to make one flower
prepare six matching hexagons and one
contrasting hexagon. You will need 25
flowers. Set the remaining hexagons aside
for later.

STARTING A HEXAGON FLOWER

2 Take the centre hexagon and place it,
right sides together, with one of the six
matching hexagons petals. Join the first
petal to the centre hexagon at just one side
edge using small oversew stitches.

ADDING THE SECOND PETAL TO THE FLOWER

3 Open out the two joined patches and
using the same method as before, stitch
the second petal to the next right edge
of the central hexagon.

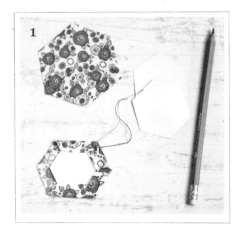

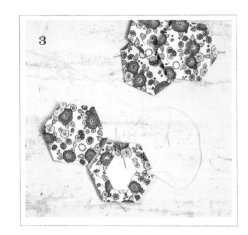

SEWING THE SECOND PETAL TO THE FIRST

4 Now fold the centre hexagon in half so that the two petals lie face to face. Bring the needle up at the point where all three patches meet and stitch the two petals together using small oversew stitches.

ADDING THE REMAINING PETALS

5 Sew on the remaining four petals from right to left in the same way to complete. Repeat for the remaining flowers.

MAKING THE HALF FLOWERS

6 Use the remaining petals to make six half flowers. These are made up of four matching 'petals' around one side of the centre hexagon.

PLANNING THE PATCHWORK LAYOUT

7 On a large flat surface, arrange the completed patchwork flowers into seven rows, starting with a top row of four, then alternating lines of three and four until you reach the last row of four. Position the part flowers at each end of the rows of three, so that the open petals and centre piece sit on the outer edge. When you are satisifed with the balance of pattern and colour, number the back of each flower so you can join them in the correct order. Now arrange the cream background hexagons all around the flowers and in the gaps to create a solid rectangle.

ADDING THE BACKGROUND HEXAGONS

8 Using the method shown in steps 2–5, oversew 12 cream hexagons around the first flower positioned at the top left-hand corner of the patchwork so that the flower is completely enclosed. Add the next flower to the right-hand side of the first, and add a further 9 cream hexagons to create the background border around this flower. Add the remaining flowers and cream hexagons to complete the top row. Continue to sew on the rest of the flowers and background hexagons one row at a time, working from left to right. When all the hexagons have been joined, unpick the tacking stitches and carefully remove the backing papers from each patch.

MAKING THE GINGHAM BORDER

9 Right sides facing, pin a short and a long gingham strip together at one end. Draw a 45 degree angle from the corner, to create a diagonal edge and stitch along this line, leaving 1.5cm free at each end. This will make a mitred corner. Open out and repeat with the other long and short strip then sew the pieces together to make a frame. Press under 1.5cm around the inside edge. Repeat to make a second frame.

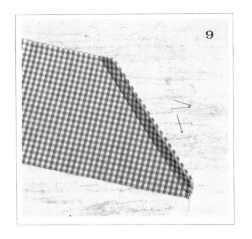

ASSEMBLING THE PATCHWORK THROW

10 Lay the Boo fabric panel right side up and place one gingham frame centrally over the top and pin to hold. Slide the ric rac over the join and topstitch in place.

11 With right sides together, align the raw edges of the second frame with the backing. Stitch around the outside edge, 1cm in. Turn right side out and press.

12 Slip the quilt wadding inbetween the two frames to create the central layer. With right side up, place the patchwork top centrally in the frame and slip stitch through the layers, all the way around the hexagons to create a zigzag edge.

Pirate Play Tent

Approximately 4m (this will
   depend on the size of your table)
   x 120cm of furnishing weight
   cream fabric
2m green bias binding
1m dark green cotton (136cm
   wide)
Approx 4m green ric rac (this will
   depend on the size of your table)
Scraps of plain and spot print
   cotton for the bunting
1m x 50cm black cotton
2 or 3 pairs of old denim jeans
2m soft red 6mm-wide cord
50cm yellow 8mm-wide cord
2 D-rings or brass loops
Matching sewing thread
50cm x 50cm fusible bonding web
Basic sewing kit
Templates: Flag, anchor and
   bunting (see page 140)

Cutting out

Measure the length, width and height of
your table and use these measurements to
cut out the fabric pieces

from cream fabric (for the tent)

   2 sides: length + 5cm x height + 5cm
   1 end: width + 5cm x height + 5cm
   1 door: width + 5cm x height
   1 door top: width + 5cm x 8cm
   4 pleats: 30cm x height + 5cm
   1 top: length + 5cm x width + 5cm

from green fabric (for the border)

   2 side borders: length + 5cm x 10cm
   1 end border: length + 5cm x 10cm
   1 door border: length + 5cm x 10cm
   4 pleat borders: 30cm x 10cm
   Two 15cm-diameter circles (for the
   portholes)

from denim

(Join the pieces to get the correct length,
incorporating the double seams)
   Four 110cm x 10cm strips (for
   the boat)
   One 50cm x 7cm strip (for the mast)
   One 40cm x 3cm strip (for the
   flagpole)
   One 30cm x 25cm strip (for the
   anchor)

from black cotton

   Five 38cm x 5cm strips (for the
   struts)

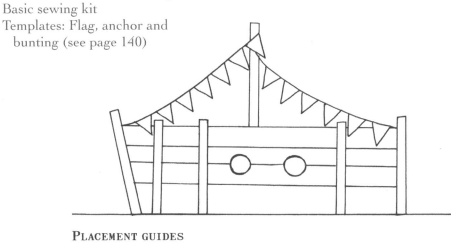

PLACEMENT GUIDES

ADDING THE BORDERS

1 Line up and pin the green pleat borders to the wrong side of the cream pleats along the bottom edge. Machine stitch in place leaving a 1.5cm seam. Fold the borders over to the right side and press. Stitch in place along the top edge then conceal the stitch line with a length of ric rac, making a 1cm notch at the centre of each top edge. Edge the door and one of the side panels in the same way.

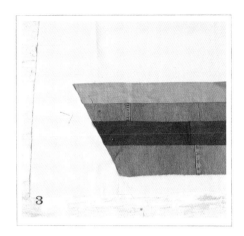

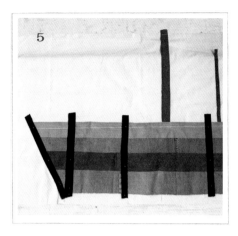

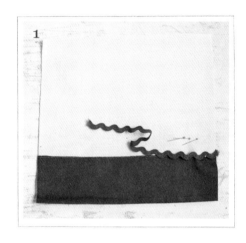

CONSTRUCTING THE BOAT

2 Join the long sides of the four denim strips with a 1.5cm seam and press the seam allowances to one side. Along the bottom edge, mark a point 10cm in from the left corner. Rule a diagonal line from this point to the top left corner. Cut along the line.

3 Press a 1.5cm turning along the top edge of the denim, then pin the boat centrally to one of the side pieces of the cream tent, 5cm up from the bottom edge.

4 Press under a 1cm turning along each long edge of the denim mast and flagpole. Pin the mast at the centre point of the top of the boat, tucking the bottom end underneath the boat. Pin the flagpole 25cm to the right of this, again tucking under the end. Sew along the top edge of the boat, then sew down both strips.

5 Neaten the struts by pressing under 1cm along one short edge and both long edges. Pin the struts down following the placement guide on page 116, so that the neatened short edges project 3cm above the top edge of the boat. Don't worry that the bottom edges of the struts look uneven. Sew the struts in place along each folded edge, 3mm in from the sides.

6 Add the green border and ric rac along the bottom edge as for the pleats shown in step 1, covering up the raw edges of the bottom of the boat and the struts.

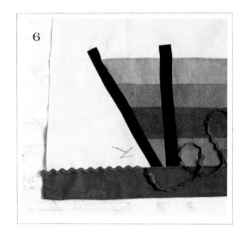

MAKING THE PORTHOLES

7 You can either stitch the two green portholes to the boat using the placement guide on page 116 or, if you want open peepholes use an air-erasable pen to draw two 9cm circles on the boat. Stitch around the lines, then cut out the centres, 3mm from the stitching.

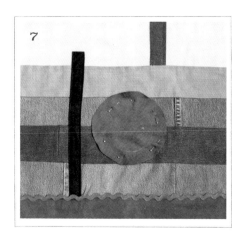

ADDING THE FLAG AND BUNTING

8 Make up the flag as for the Clubhouse Flag on page 68. Pin to the top of the flagpole and sew around the edge using a black zigzag stitch.

9 Sew together three lines of bunting, made of 6, 7 and 8 pennants, using the template on page 140 and following the instructions for the Nature Walk Bunting on page 24. Trim 1cm from the top of each pennant before making up and keep a 15cm length of binding free at each end.

10 Pin the 7-pennant bunting to the left side of the boat, from the edge of the boat and prow to the top right-hand side of the mast. Pin the 6-pennant bunting to the right side of the boat, from the top left of the side of the mast to the edge of the boat and the stern. Stitch in place along the bias binding.

MAKING THE DOOR

11 Make a 2cm double hem at each long edge of the door. Trace the anchor on page 140 onto bonding web, cut out roughly and press onto the denim. Trim around the outline, peel off the backing and press to the right corner of the cream door, 5cm up from the bottom edge and at a slight angle. Edge with a blue zigzag stitch.

12 Arrange the length of cord in a series of curves and loops (using the placement drawing on page 116 as a guide) using scissors to pierce holes through the fabric where necessary. Pin and hand stitch down. Stitch the remaining 8-pennant length of bunting, to loop over the cord.

13 Cut the yellow cord in two and loop one piece through each D-ring and pull tight. Pin the raw ends of each to a top corner of the door, 2cm in from the outside edge. Align and stitch the door top to the edge of the door with a 1cm seam. Hem the side edges in line with the door. Sew the top of the door to one end of the top panel with a 1cm seam. Cut two 20cm lengths from the remaining yellow cord and sew one to each side edge of the door, 50cm from the bottom and on the wrong side. Keep the door open by rolling it up and securing the ties to the metal loops.

MAKING UP

14 Sew a pleat to each edge of the two boat sides, with right sides facing. Sew the end panel between the two to make a continuous length.

15 Pin the top edge of the end panel to the opposite end of the top panel with right sides facing. Pin the top edges of the two boat sides to the long edges. Pin the notches at the top of the pleats to the four corners. Pin down the surplus fabric at the top of the pleats. At the door end, pin the edges of the pleats over the top edge of the door. Tack all round, then machine stitch 15mm from the edge.

Techniques

All of the basic techniques that you'll need to make the Belle & Boo sewing projects, from the Nature Walk Bunting (page 24) to the Pirate Play Tent (page 116) are illustrated here: including seaming, hemming, binding and simple embroidery stitches. You'll find that anything else that you need to know will be explained in the step-by-step project instructions.

Embroidery

TRANSFERRING OUTLINES

There are several ways to transfer a template onto fabric, but this is the most straightforward. Photocopy or trace the image onto dressmaker's paper and cut out. Draw around the outside edge with a sharp pencil or an air-erasable pen – this gives a line that will disappear over time. Add in the details, referring back to the original template.

MOUNTING IN A HOOP

Keeping the fabric taut within an embroidery hoop will help to keep all of your embroidery stitches neat and regular. Unscrew the two halves of the frame and place the fabric over the inside ring. Place the other ring on top and push it down. Pull the fabric evenly all the way around to increase the tension. Tighten the screw to hold in place.

STRAIGHT STITCH

This is the simplest embroidery stitch. Single straight stitches are used for details and broken outlines whilst straight stitches that are placed close together can be used to quickly fill areas with solid blocks of colour. These stitches can be made at any length and in any direction. Vary the length of the stitches to give more texture.

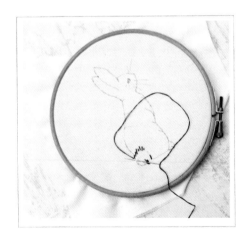

STEM STITCH

This is good for when making outlines: make all the stitches regular for a smooth line, or uneven for a softer, hand-drawn feel. Make a straight stitch from left to right, and then come back up directly alongside and halfway down the previous stitch to make the next. Repeat to the end.

SATIN STITCH

Satin stitch is made up of rows of single vertical straight stitches, worked tightly alongside each other to give a smooth, satiny surface. Create a more random look by working the second row of encroaching satin stitch so that it overlaps the first and angle the stitches to fit within the outline.

BUTTONHOLE LOOP

This old-fashioned fastening loop is perfect for the tiny envelope on the Tooth Fairy Pillow (page 54). It is similar to blanket stitch but has an extra twist which gives it a firmer edge. Make four fairly loose straight stitches as the foundation bar. Hold the needle under the bar and loop the thread behind it from left to right. Pull the needle through over the thread and gently pull the thread up and back to make a small 'purl' on the outside edge. Practice on spare fabric first and you'll find that this is much easier to do than it is to describe!

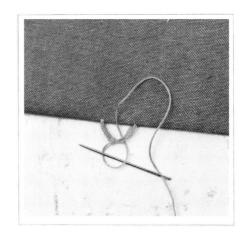

BACK STITCH

This stitch gives a neat line. Work from right to left. Start with a small backwards stitch from left to right then bring the needle up at the left, leaving a space equal to the first stitch. Take the thread back to the end of the previous stitch. Repeat.

BLANKET STITCH

This is a useful stitch for defining edges and joining layers. Always leave a space between stitches. Push the needle halfway into the fabric and place the length of thread under the needle tip. Draw tight to create a loop at the edge and repeat.

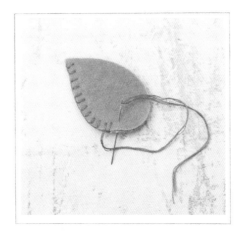

Hems

SINGLE HEM

With the wrong side of the fabric facing you, turn up the bottom edge (and the sides if required) to the depth given in the steps. Use a tape measure to check the hem is the same length all the way along, then tack, pin or press as directed. Stitch in place by hand or machine, 3–4mm from the raw edge.

DOUBLE HEM

Make and press a single turning as for a single hem, then fold back a second turning to the depth given. Make sure it is the same all the way along and machine stitch 3–4mm from the inside fold. Finish off the Clubhouse Flag (page 68) in this way, so that it looks neat from both sides.

BIAS BINDING

Thicker fabrics, which are too bulky to fold, can be finished with ready-made bias binding. There are two methods of doing this: the Little Helper Apron (page 18) has slotted-over binding and the Explorer's Satchel (page 62) has turned binding, which will give a stitch-free look.

1 For the first method, simply fold the binding strip in half lengthways with the raw edges on the inside and slip it over the raw edge. Tack through all the layers and stitch in place 2–3mm from the edge.

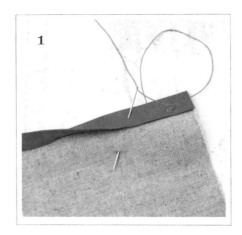

2 For the second method, open out one fold of the binding and with right sides facing, pin the raw edge along the edge of the fabric. Machine stitch along the fold. Turn the binding to the other side and tack down the fold, making sure that it lies over and covers the seam line. Sew down from the right side, stitching 'in the ditch': directly over the join between the binding and the fabric.

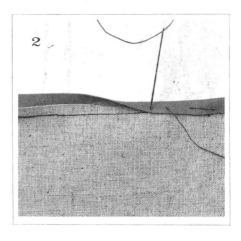

Seams

SINGLE SEAM

1 Pin the two fabric edges that are to be joined together, with the right sides facing. Machine stitch parallel to the edges, using the side of the presser foot or the lines on the sewing machine bed to keep the seam allowance even.

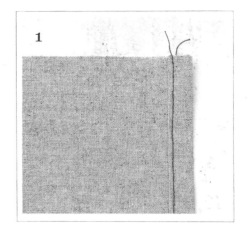

2 'Press open' by parting the two seams with the tip of the iron and press flat.

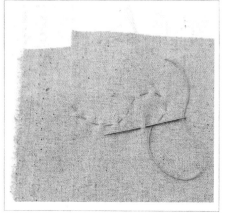

Hand Stitching

RUNNING STITCH

Large, evenly spaced running stitches can be used for tacking two pieces of fabric together as a temporary join. Smaller running stitches are used for embroidered details, or can be pulled up as a gathering stitch. The spaces between each stitch should be the same length as the stitches themselves.

CORNER SEAM

Sew along the first edge as far as the end of the seam allowance. Keeping the needle down, lift the foot and turn the fabric by ninety degrees. Lower the foot and continue along the second edge. Clip a small triangle of fabric from the corners of the seam allowance to make sure that the seam will lie flat when it is turned right side out. Clip about 3mm away from the stitch line. Sharper angles, like those on the Nature Walk Bunting pennants (page 24), will need more fabric trimmed.

OVERSEW

2 Join two folded edges, such as the hexagons from the Patchwork Bedcover (page 110), or thick fabric like the felted wool used for Boo (page 32) with this stitch. Tack or hold the two pieces together with right sides facing and sew at a right angle through both layers, close to the edge. Make another stitch in exactly the same way, and carry on to the end of the join.

SLIP STITCH

1 This stitch gives an almost invisible join when stitching together two pieces of fabric. The idea is that most of the stitch is hidden. Bring the needle 1mm from the edge of the lower piece of fabric. Insert it directly above in the other fabric and come out again 5mm along, at the same level. Make a small downwards stitch into the lower fabric and continue to the end of the seam.

ABCDE
FGHIJK
LMNOP
QRSTU
VWXYZ

Enlarge your chosen initial by 400%

POCKET POSITION

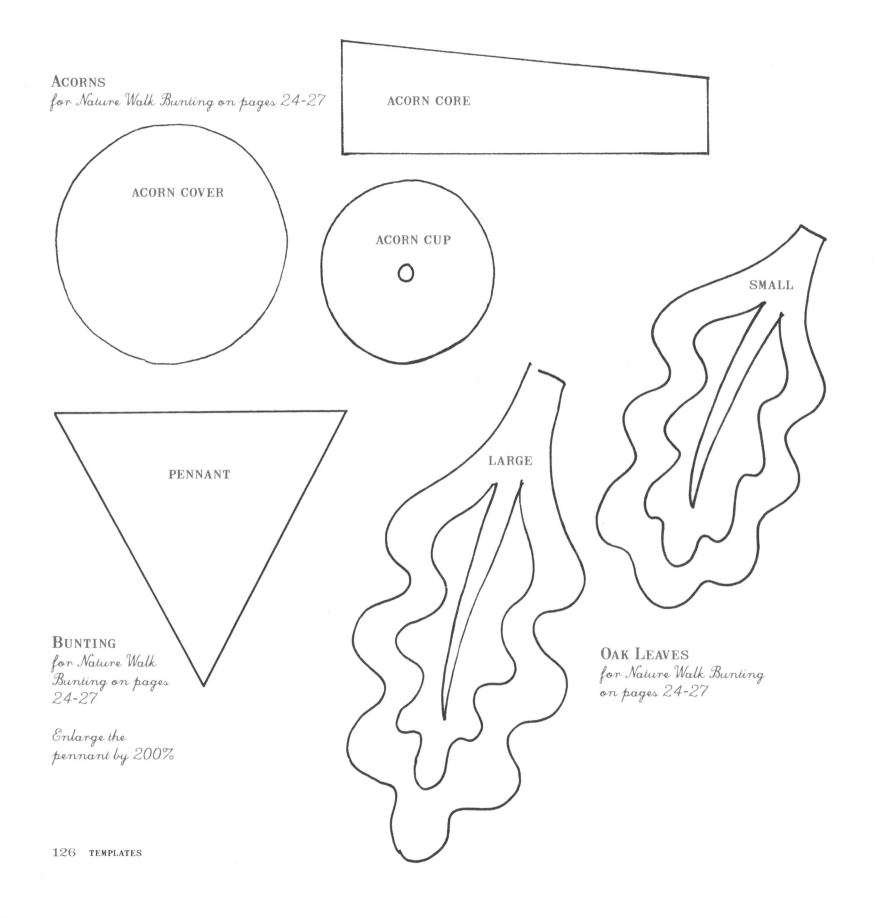

ACORNS
for Nature Walk Bunting on pages 24-27

ACORN CORE

ACORN COVER

ACORN CUP

SMALL

PENNANT

LARGE

BUNTING
*for Nature Walk
Bunting on pages
24-27*

*Enlarge the
pennant by 200%*

OAK LEAVES
*for Nature Walk Bunting
on pages 24-27*

Boo
for Boo on pages 32-36

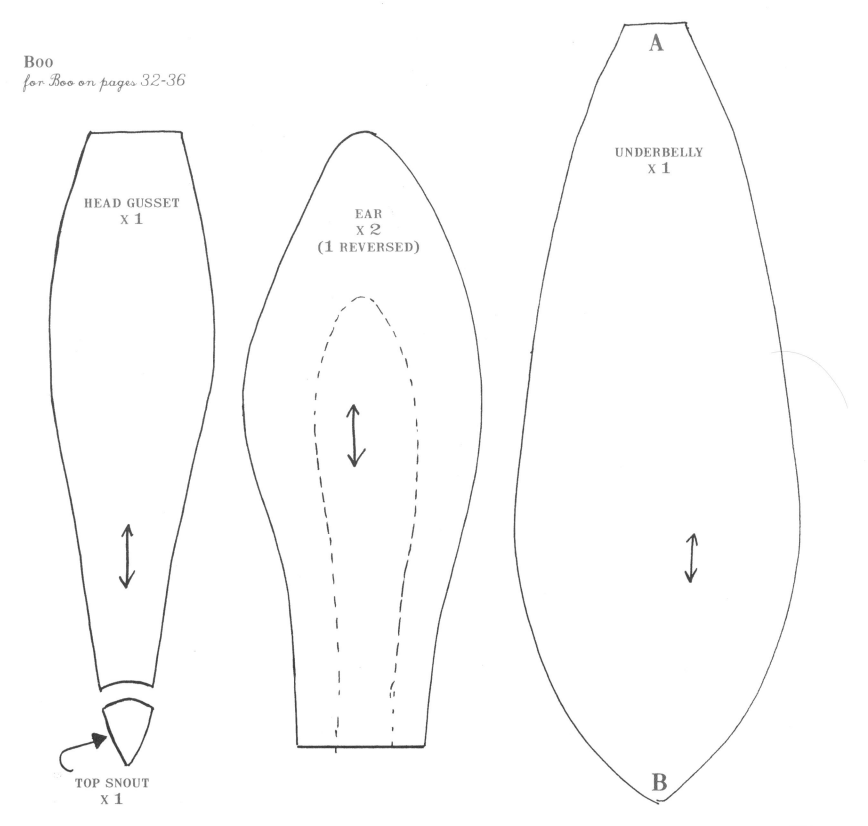

HEAD GUSSET
x 1

TOP SNOUT
x 1

EAR
x 2
(1 REVERSED)

A

UNDERBELLY
x 1

B

BOO CONTINUED
for Boo on pages 32-36

SIDE SNOUT
x 2
(1 REVERSED)

NOSE
x 1

SIDE HEAD
x 2
(1 REVERSED)

EYE
x 2
(1 REVERSED)

A

BODY
x 2
(1 REVERSED)

FRONT

B

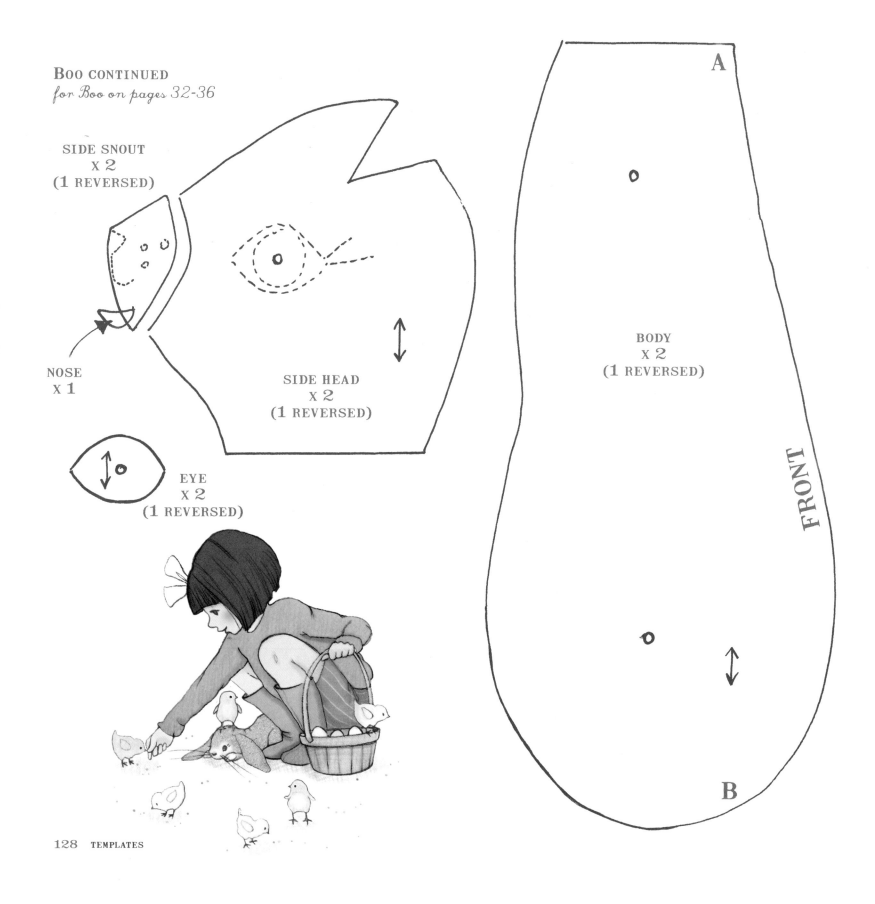

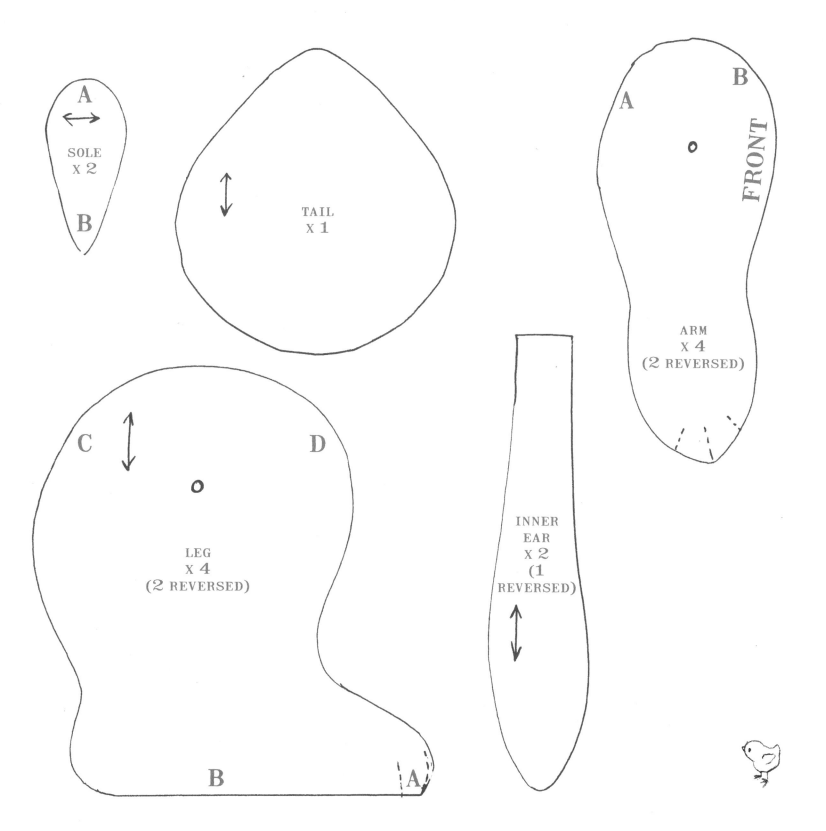

A

SOLE
x 2

B

TAIL
x 1

A

B

FRONT

ARM
x 4
(2 REVERSED)

C

D

LEG
x 4
(2 REVERSED)

B

A

INNER
EAR
x 2
(1
REVERSED)

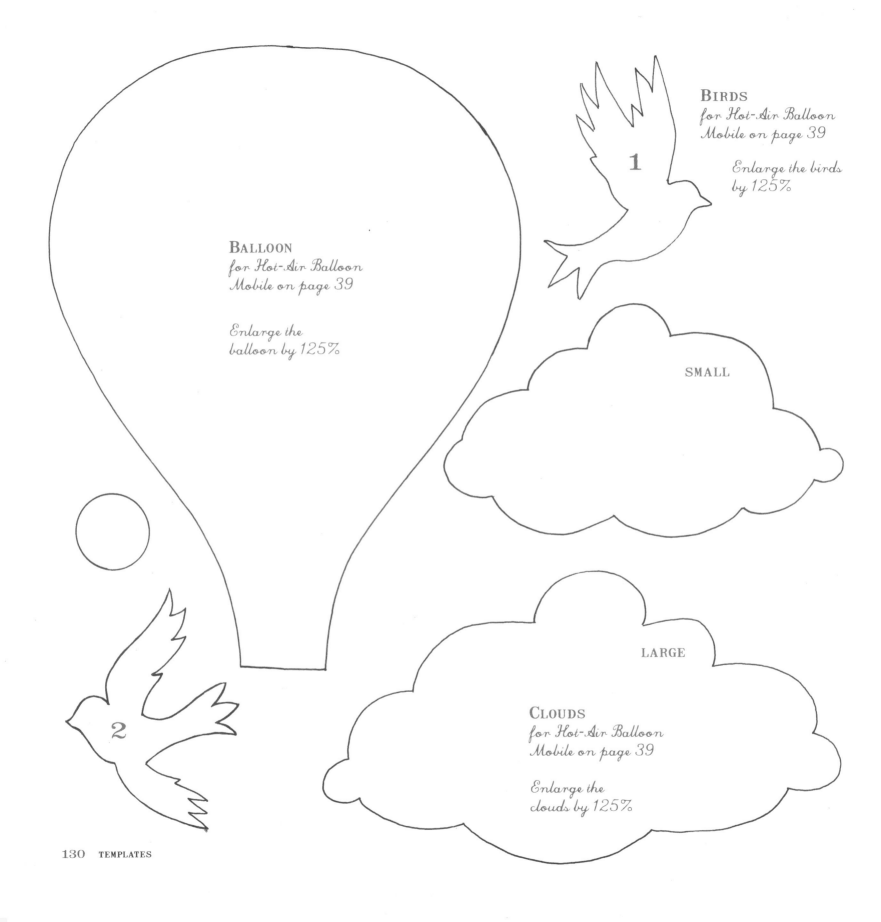

BIRDS
for Hot-Air Balloon
Mobile on page 39

Enlarge the birds
by 125%

1

BALLOON
for Hot-Air Balloon
Mobile on page 39

Enlarge the
balloon by 125%

SMALL

2

LARGE

CLOUDS
for Hot-Air Balloon
Mobile on page 39

Enlarge the
clouds by 125%

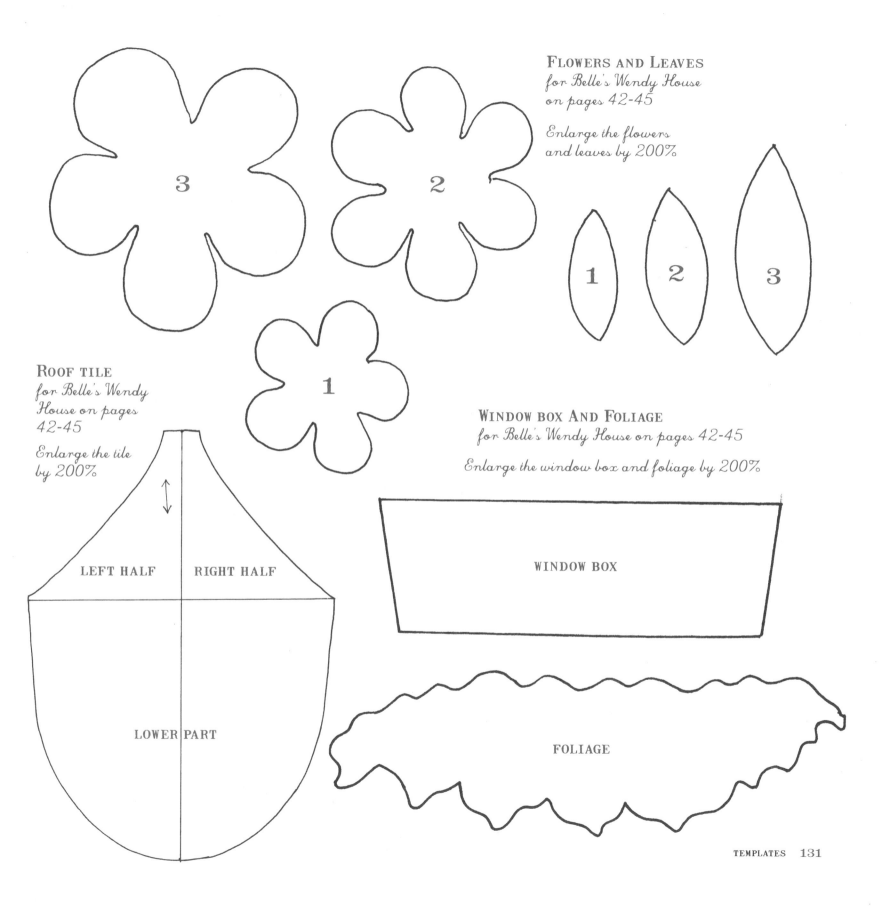

FLOWERS AND LEAVES
*for Belle's Wendy House
on pages 42-45*

*Enlarge the flowers
and leaves by 200%*

3

2

1

2

3

ROOF TILE
*for Belle's Wendy
House on pages
42-45*

*Enlarge the tile
by 200%*

1

LEFT HALF   RIGHT HALF

LOWER PART

WINDOW BOX AND FOLIAGE
for Belle's Wendy House on pages 42-45

Enlarge the window box and foliage by 200%

WINDOW BOX

FOLIAGE

BOO EMBROIDERY
for Tooth Fairy Pillow
on pages 54-57

POCKET
for Tooth Fairy Pillow on pages 54-57

POCKET
x 2

NUMBERS
for Hopscotch Mat on pages 59-60

Enlarge each number by 250%

SKULL
for Clubhouse
Flag on page 68

NUMBERS
for Quiet Book on pages 74-81

HOUSE
for Quiet Book on pages 74-81

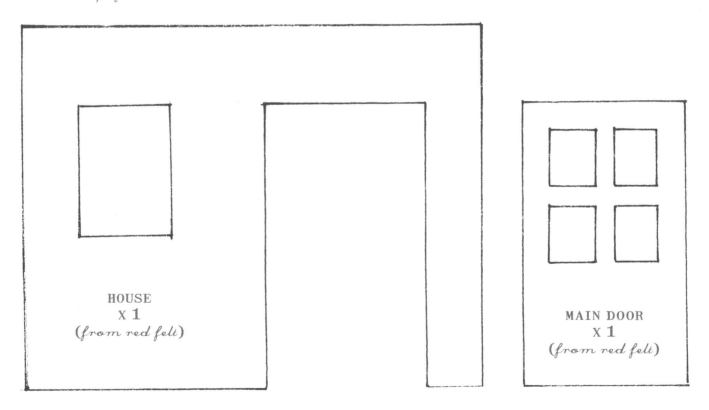

**HOUSE
x 1**
(from red felt)

**MAIN DOOR
x 1**
(from red felt)

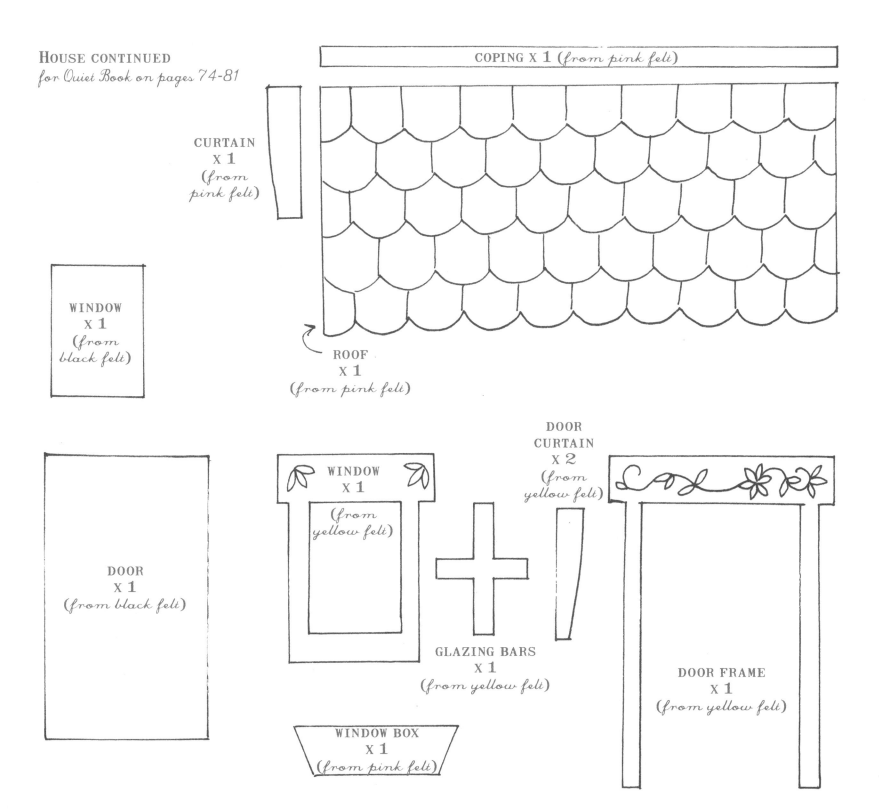

HOUSE CONTINUED
for Quiet Book on pages 74-81

COPING X 1 (from pink felt)

CURTAIN
x 1
(from
pink felt)

WINDOW
X 1
(from
black felt)

ROOF
X 1
(from pink felt)

DOOR
x 1
(from black felt)

WINDOW
X 1
(from
yellow felt)

GLAZING BARS
x 1
(from yellow felt)

WINDOW BOX
X 1
(from pink felt)

DOOR
CURTAIN
X 2
(from
yellow felt)

DOOR FRAME
x 1
(from yellow felt)

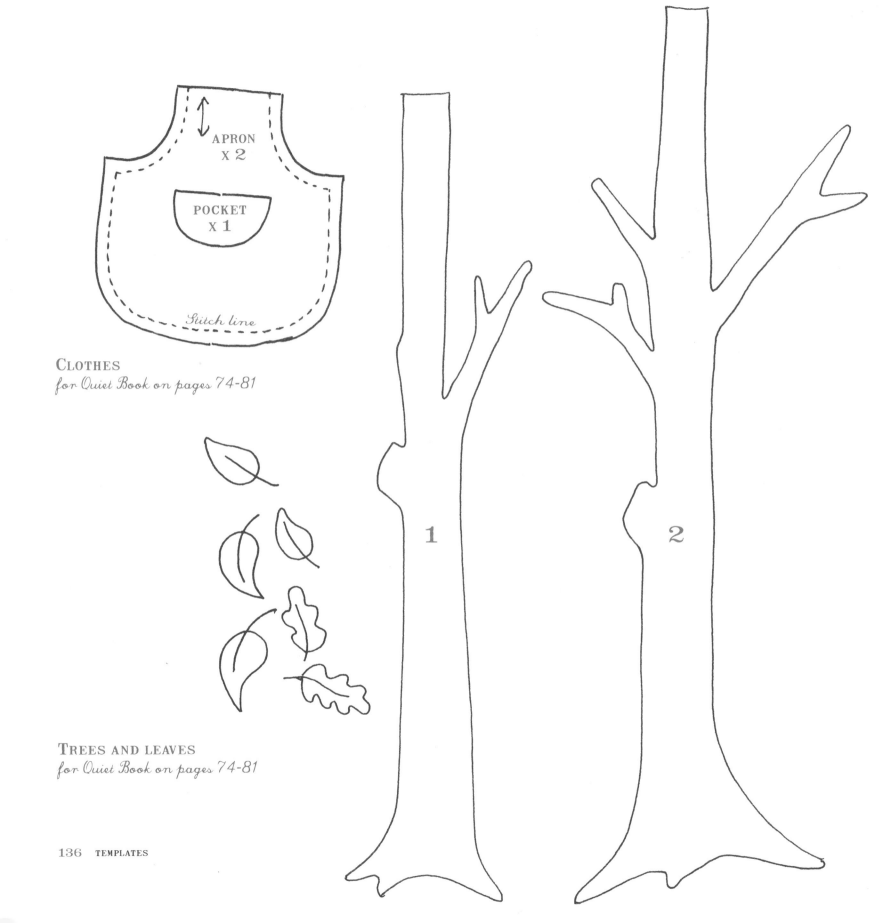

APRON
x 2

POCKET
x 1

Stitch line

CLOTHES
for Quiet Book on pages 74–81

TREES AND LEAVES
for Quiet Book on pages 74–81

1

2

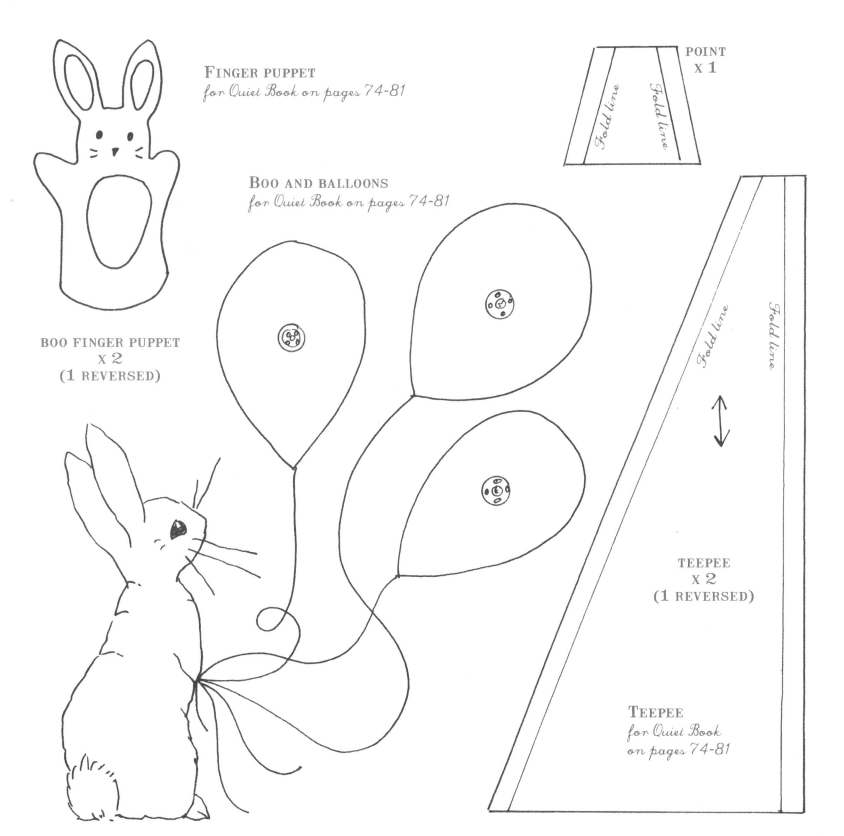

FINGER PUPPET
for Quiet Book on pages 74-81

BOO AND BALLOONS
for Quiet Book on pages 74-81

BOO FINGER PUPPET
x 2
(1 REVERSED)

POINT
X 1

Fold line   *Fold line*

Fold line   *Fold line*

TEEPEE
x 2
(1 REVERSED)

TEEPEE
*for Quiet Book
on pages 74-81*

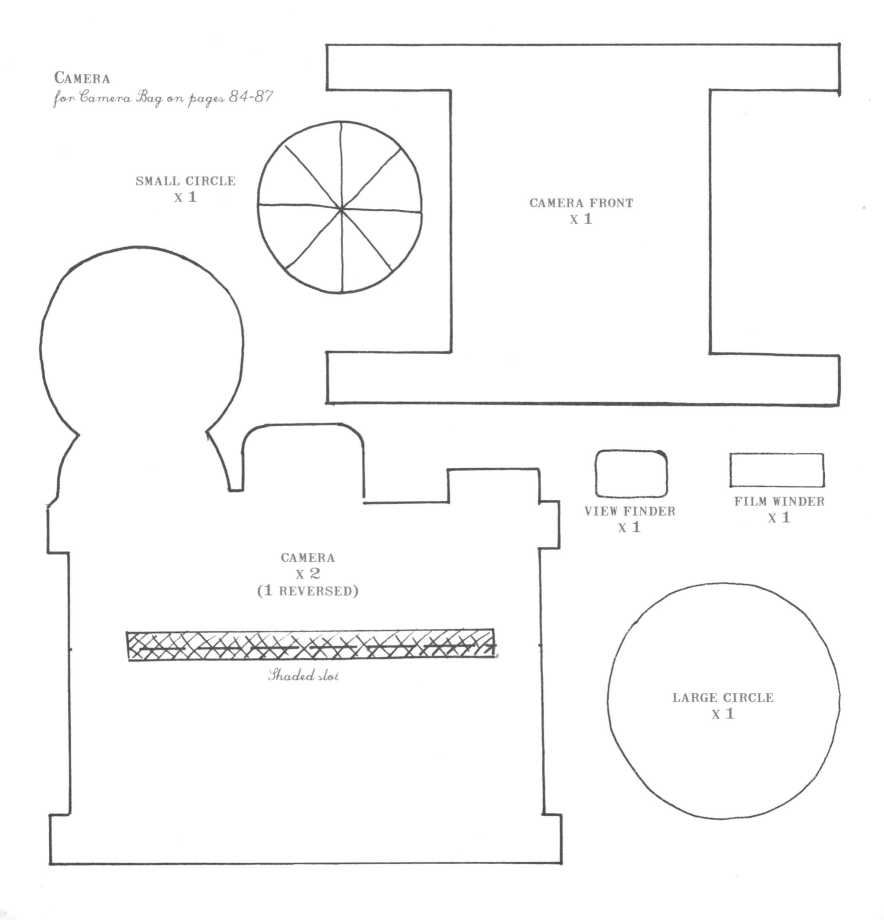

CAMERA
for Camera Bag on pages 84-87

SMALL CIRCLE
x 1

CAMERA FRONT
x 1

VIEW FINDER
x 1

FILM WINDER
x 1

CAMERA
x 2
(1 REVERSED)

Shaded slot

LARGE CIRCLE
x 1

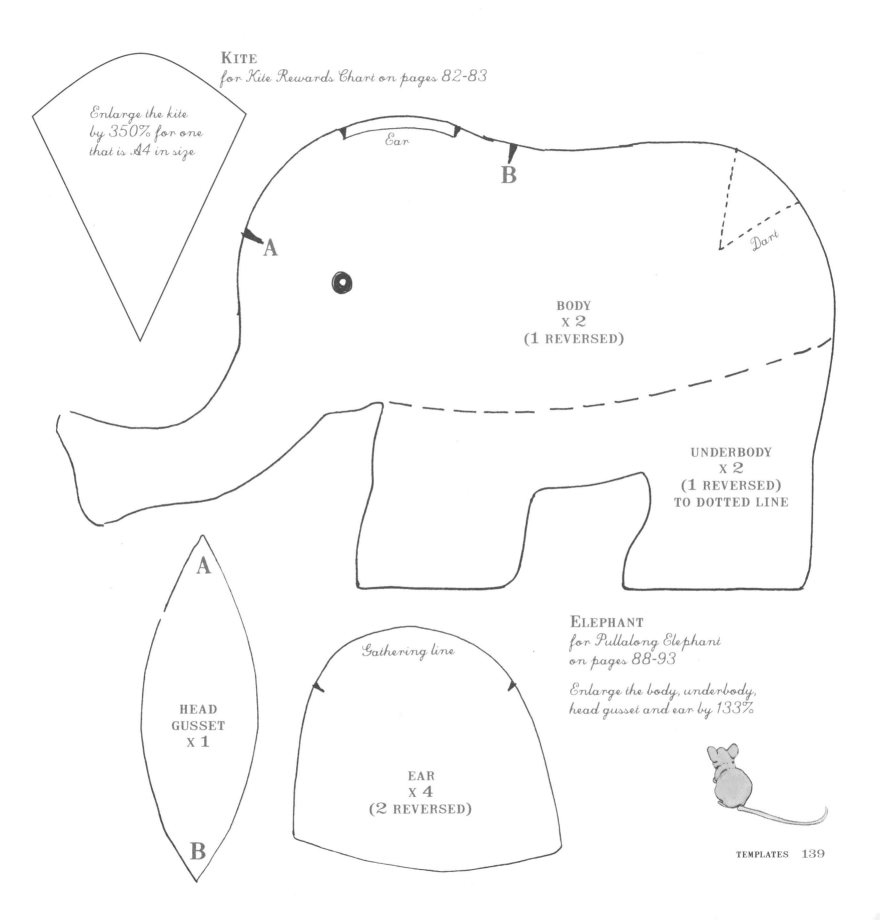

KITE
for Kite Rewards Chart on pages 82-83

Enlarge the kite by 350% for one that is A4 in size

Ear

B

A

Dart

**BODY
x 2
(1 REVERSED)**

**UNDERBODY
x 2
(1 REVERSED)
TO DOTTED LINE**

A

B

**HEAD
GUSSET
x 1**

Gathering line

**EAR
x 4
(2 REVERSED)**

ELEPHANT
for Pullalong Elephant on pages 88-93

Enlarge the body, underbody, head gusset and ear by 133%

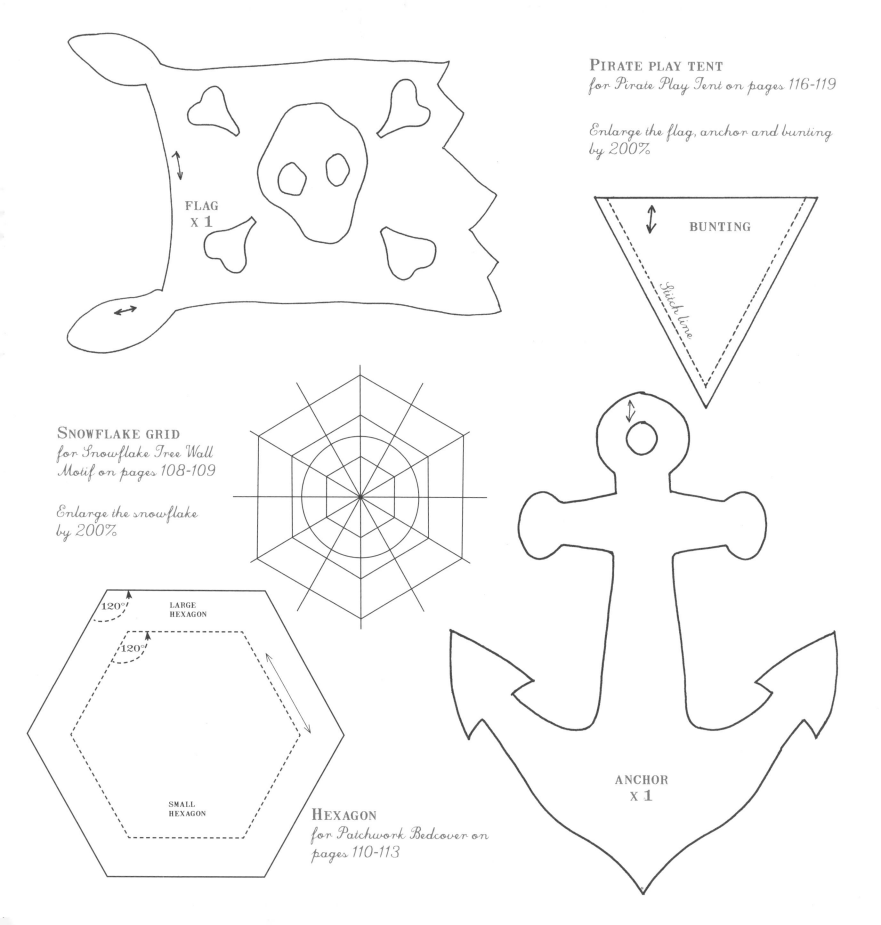

FLAG
x 1

PIRATE PLAY TENT
for Pirate Play Tent on pages 116–119

Enlarge the flag, anchor and bunting by 200%

BUNTING

Stitch line

SNOWFLAKE GRID
for Snowflake Tree Wall Motif on pages 108–109

Enlarge the snowflake by 200%

120°   LARGE
        HEXAGON

120°

SMALL
HEXAGON

HEXAGON
for Patchwork Bedcover on pages 110–113

ANCHOR
x 1

Index

PROJECTS CONCEIVED AND MADE BY
Lucinda Ganderton and Lisa Pendreigh

PUBLISHING DIRECTOR Jane O'Shea
CREATIVE DIRECTOR Helen Lewis
COMMISSIONING EDITOR Lisa Pendreigh
ART DIRECTION AND DESIGN Claire Peters
EDITOR Louise McKeever
ILLUSTRATOR Mandy Sutcliffe
PHOTOGRAPHER Laura Edwards
STYLIST Polly Webb-Wilson
MODELS Bodhi; Meadow at Bruce and Brown
PRODUCTION DIRECTOR Vincent Smith
PRODUCTION CONTROLLER Leonie Kellman

Quadrille
craft

www.quadrillecraft.co.uk

First published in 2013 by
Quadrille Publishing Ltd
Alhambra House
27–31 Charing Cross Road
London WC2H 0LS
www.quadrille.co.uk

British Library Cataloguing-in-Publication Data.
A catalogue record for this book is available from the
British Library.

ISBN: 978 184949 267 6

Printed in China

uppliers

ARTHUR BEALE
Stocks: nautical cord.
194 Shaftesbury Avenue
London WC2H 8JP
020 7836 9034

BELLE & BOO
0117 924 6382
hello@belleandboo.com
www.belleandboo.com

CLOTH HOUSE
47 Berwick Street
London W1F 8SJ
020 7437 5155
info@clothhouse.com
www.clothhouse.net

DEBBIE BLISS
www.debbieblissonline.com

DMC CREATIVE WORLD
0116 275 4000
www.dmccreative.co.uk

E-CRAFTS
Stocks: safety toy eyes and joints.
01384 230 000
sales@e-crafts.co.uk
www.e-crafts.co.uk

HARTS OF HERTFORD
14 Bull Plain
Hertford SG14 1DT
01992 558 106
info@hartsofhertford.co.uk
www.hartsofhertford.co.uk

HOBBYCRAFT
01202 596 100
www.hobbycraft.co.uk

JAFFE ET FILS LTD
Stocks: feathers.
0129 733 408
info@jaffefeathers.co.uk
www.jaffefeathers.co.uk

JOHN LEWIS
Stocks: bean bag liners and beads.
Oxford Street
London W1A 1EX
and branches nationwide
08456 049 049
www.johnlewis.com

KLEINS
5 Noel Street
London W1F 8GD
020 7437 6162
www.kleins.co.uk

MACCULLOCH & WALLIS
25–26 Dering Street
London W1S 1AT
020 7629 0311
mailorder@macculloch.com
www.macculloch-wallis.co.uk

THE MAKERY EMPORIUM
16 Northumberland Place
Bath, Avon BA1 5AR
01225 487 708
kate@themakeryonline.co.uk
www.themakeryonline.co.uk

MANDORS
134 Renfrew Street
Glasgow G3 6ST
01413 327 716
fabric@mandors.co.uk
www.mandors.co.uk

MILLIE MOON
24–25 Catherine Hill
Frome, Somerset BA11 1BY
01373 464 650
info@milliemoonshop.co.uk
www.milliemoonshop.co.uk

NUTSCENE
Stocks: Nutscene Jute 3ply garden twine.
01307 468 589
sales@nutscene.com
www.nutscene.com

OUR PATTERNED HAND
49 Broadway Market
London E8 4PH
020 7812 9912
ours@ourpatternedhand.co.uk
www.ourpatternedhand.co.uk

SOAP BASICS
Stocks: soap base, colour and fragance.
01225 899 286
info@soapbasics.com
www.soapbasics.com

TIKKI
Stocks: fabric and ric rac.
020 8948 8462
info@tikkilondon.com
www.tikkilondon.com

WOODWARD PDA LTD
Stocks: coloured card.
01773 712 266
pda@pdacardandcraft.co.uk
www.PDAcardandcraft.co.uk

WOOL FELT COMPANY
Stocks: coloured felt.
www.woolfeltcompany.co.uk

YEOMAN'S YARN
Stocks: yarn, including Cotton Cannele.
01162 404 464
sales@yeomanyarns.co.uk
www.yeoman-yarns.co.uk